PRAISE FOR
FRIEND OF SINNERS

"Rich Wilkerson Jr. has inspired and deepened my walk with Christ in his new book *Friend of Sinners*. While it is easy for Christians today to be labeled as judgmental, this book shows how Jesus lived as a friend to the outcast and gives you a strategy to live your life in the same way."

—Mark Batterson, pastor and *New York Times*
bestselling author of *The Circle Maker*

"Most people know some facts and information about Jesus: carpenter, teacher, miracle worker. But it's how we know him personally that makes all the difference. Rich Wilkerson Jr.'s new book, *Friend of Sinners* will challenge you to take a step back, question your approach, and begin choosing relationship over routine religion."

—Steven Furtick, pastor of Elevation Church
and *New York Times* bestselling author

"*Friend of Sinners* highlights a core truth this world needs to hear—we must break out of the boxes of our normality and dare to go close to those we don't understand. Pastor Rich beautifully emphasizes this while encouraging us to start where people are, not where we want them to be. This book will forever change how you love others."

—Lysa TerKeurst, *New York Times* bestselling
author and president of Proverbs 31 Ministries

"Rich carries the ability to seamlessly engage people with the message of Jesus, reaching the church and unchurched, both saved and sinners alike. He is a generational thinker, planner, and writer in addition to being a phenomenal pastor. Friendship with God through Christ is both a simple, yet a profoundly important foundation that is at the very core of our faith. Inspiring and thought-provoking, *Friend of Sinners* unpacks friendship with Jesus in a refreshing and transforming way."

—Brian Houston, senior pastor and gobal
founder of Hillsong Church

FRIEND

OF

SINNERS

FRIEND OF SINNERS

Why Jesus Cares More About
Relationship Than Perfection

RICH WILKERSON, JR.

NELSON
BOOKS

An Imprint of Thomas Nelson

Published in Nashville, Tennessee, by Nelson Books, an imprint of Thomas Nelson. Nelson Books and Thomas Nelson are registered trademarks of HarperCollins Christian Publishing, Inc.

Published in association with the literary agency of The Fedd Agency, Inc., P.O. Box 341973, Austin, Texas, 78734.

Thomas Nelson titles may be purchased in bulk for educational, business, fund-raising, or sales promotional use. For information, please e-mail SpecialMarkets@ ThomasNelson.com.

Any Internet addresses, phone numbers, or company or product information printed in this book are offered as a resource and are not intended in any way to be or to imply an endorsement by Thomas Nelson, nor does Thomas Nelson vouch for the existence, content, or services of these sites, phone numbers, companies, or products beyond the life of this book.

Unless otherwise noted, Scripture quotations are taken from the Holy Bible, New International Version®, NIV®. Copyright © 1973, 1978, 1984, 2011 by Biblica, Inc.® Used by permission of Zondervan. All rights reserved worldwide. www.zondervan.com. The "NIV" and "New International Version" are trademarks registered in the United States Patent and Trademark Office by Biblica, Inc.®

Scripture quotations marked NLT are taken from the *Holy Bible*, New Living Translation. © 1996, 2004, 2007, 2013 by Tyndale House Foundation. Used by permission of Tyndale House Publishers, Inc., Carol Stream, Illinois 60188. All rights reserved.

Scripture quotations marked ESV are taken from the ESV® Bible (The Holy Bible, English Standard Version®). Copyright © 2001 by Crossway, a publishing ministry of Good News Publishers. Used by permission. All rights reserved.

Scripture quotations marked NKJV are taken from the New King James Version®. © 1982 by Thomas Nelson. Used by permission. All rights reserved.

Scripture quotations marked THE MESSAGE are taken from *The Message*. Copyright © by Eugene H. Peterson 1993, 1994, 1995, 1996, 2000, 2001, 2002. Used by permission of Tyndale House Publishers, Inc.

ISBN 978-0-7180-3271-5 (eBook)

Library of Congress Cataloging-in-Publication Data

ISBN 978–0–7180-3270-8
Library of Congress Control Number: 2017952466

Printed in the United States of America

18 19 20 21 22 LSC 10 9 8 7 6 5 4 3 2 1

To my firstborn son, our miracle in motion.
You're my brave boy.
You were worth the wait.

CONTENTS

INTRODUCTION

I DIDN'T REALLY HAVE A NICKNAME AS A child—I was Richie until high school, then Rich ever since. There was one exception, though. On the desperate battleground that was junior high dodgeball, I earned a nickname I'm still rather proud of: *Richie Rampage.*

It wasn't just a nickname. It was more of an alter ego. A superpower, even. When the game started, I was always calm, cool, suave. But when the competition hit a certain level, something inside me would snap. My friends could always tell the moment it happened. "Look out, Richie Rampage is back!"

My eyes would narrow. My senses would become heightened. Any trace of humor or humanity would disappear. I was a machine, a survivor, a pro. Suddenly, I could catch every ball thrown my way, and I could fire the ball back with insane precision and speed. My opponents could only limp off, bruised and beaten.

Time and wishful thinking have probably exaggerated the legend of Richie Rampage, to be honest. But my nickname communicated something about me, about how people saw me. That's the nature of nicknames. What people call you says a lot about how they perceive you. And sometimes their perception can be very revealing.

Jesus was called a lot of names. All he did was love and help people, yet he had his share of bullies and critics. Many of the religious leaders of the day were jealous of his success and afraid he would upset the status quo. They wanted to discredit him in the eyes of the public, so they said all sorts of crazy things about him. They whispered that he was an illegitimate child. They accused him of being demon-possessed. They denounced him to the Roman authorities as a rioter, a threat to public peace.

Jesus didn't deserve the hate, but it turns out one of their nicknames for him was true. They called him "a friend of tax collectors and sinners" (Luke 7:34 ESV). In their minds, that was one of the greatest indictments imaginable. Jesus hung out with bad people, therefore he must be bad too. That was their logic.

But for Jesus, the title *Friend of Sinners* was a sign of success, not a source of shame. I can imagine him smiling the first time he heard the phrase. "Friend of sinners? I'll take that as a compliment." Why? Because it was the very definition of his mission.

I can't stop thinking about what Jesus' nickname means for me, for my friends, and for humanity today. What kind of God labels himself a friend of sinners? I could believe "judge of sinners"; I could even believe "Savior of sinners." But *friend*? Really?

The goal of this book is to discover the implications of this concept for you and me. Friendship is far more important to God than we often realize. We tend to think he puts top priority on performance, purity, and perfection, and we assume relationship is the eventual reward for those things. In other words, the more like Jesus we become, the closer our relationship with him will be. Actually, it works the other way around. The closer we get to Jesus, the more like him we become. Relationship comes first; change comes later. Hence the subtitle of this book: *Why Jesus Cares More About Relationship Than Perfection.*

Unfortunately, many people who consider themselves Christians and followers of Jesus mix up the order. We often try to *correct* people before we *connect* with people. Not Jesus. As we read about his life and listen to his teachings, we see time and time again a man who went out of his way to befriend people who had been ostracized, labeled, and rejected by society. Many of those people eventually became world-famous leaders in the Christian church. Some of them became writers of the New Testament. Some of them gave their lives for Jesus. What happened? What transformed them? They were friends of Jesus, and their lives were inevitably and irrevocably changed as a result.

This book is divided into three parts. Part 1, Christ, describes Jesus and his message of grace. This is the foundation for everything, because until we understand how extravagant his grace is—and how much we all need it—we won't understand why he can be a friend of sinners. Part 2, Culture, describes God's heart of love for the world. God is obsessed with lost people, and that passion drives his initiative to find and aid those who are lost. Part 3, Church, is about the mission of everyone who has become a friend of Jesus to share his love with a world in need. This is the logical result of understanding Jesus' message of grace and God's heart for the lost. When we realize how much God has done for us and how much he loves the world, we will find ourselves opening our hearts and lives to hurting people.

Oscar Wilde, the famous nineteenth-century playwright, once wrote, "Every saint has a past, and every sinner has a future."[1] In other words, even the best person needs humility, and even the worst person has hope. God cares about everyone, regardless of where they are on their journey: spiritually mature or seeker, devout or in doubt, religious or simply curious. All of us need him, and all of us can find him. Whether we consider ourselves saints or sinners, Jesus wants to be our friend. Let's take a look at what that means.

PART 1

CHRIST: THE SCANDAL
OF THE GOSPEL

I HAVE BEEN A PASTOR AND A PREACHER for quite a few years now, but in some ways I feel like I'm just starting to understand the message of Jesus. It's not that it's too complex—it isn't. It's that it is so counterculture, so counterintuitive, that it can be hard to believe.

In this section, we'll explore the message of Jesus. Sometimes we use the word *gospel*, which simply means "good news," to refer to this message. What is the gospel? What did Jesus teach? And what does that mean for us?

You might already have some answers to those questions. Chances are, those answers have a lot to do with morality and behavior, good and bad, sin and holiness, right and wrong.

That is part of his message, but it's not all of it. *And it's not the most important part.* I'd like to invite you to open your mind and heart as you read this book. I think you'll discover a different Jesus in these pages, a Jesus who will radically change the way you see God, yourself, and others.

You might not be sure what you believe about Jesus. That's fine too. You don't have to believe a certain thing or behave a certain way to be welcomed by Jesus. Come as you are, because he accepts you as you are. That's the beauty of the gospel. As you read about Jesus' message of grace, love, and friendship, I think you'll discover more about him than you ever imagined.

Jesus calls us friends, not because of who we are or what we have done, but because of who he is. He is the friend of all people, and he invites us into friendship with him.

CHAPTER 1

MISSED MESSAGE

A FEW YEARS AGO MY WIFE, DAWNCHERÉ, surprised me with a special gift for my twenty-seventh birthday. Now, let me preface this story by mentioning that DawnCheré loves surprises. She likes *being* surprised, but she especially loves *planning* surprises for others.

I, on the other hand, hate being surprised. Down deep, I have a compulsive desire to be in control. I like to have a clear plan. So surprises aren't really my thing.

Anyway, DawnCheré came home from work and handed me a box. "Babe, I got you the best gift!" She was clearly excited.

I said, "What—did you wrap yourself up, girl?"

She ignored me, which is one of her spiritual gifts. "Open the box. You're going to love it!"

I unwrapped the box and opened it. Inside was a piece of paper she had designed and printed. It said, "In two weeks I'm taking you to the Kings of Leon concert at the Bank Atlantic Center."

I was pumped. They are one of our favorite bands, and I

couldn't wait to see them live. Finally—a surprise I could get excited about!

For the next two weeks, we did what people do when they are anticipating something. We talked about it every day. "Eleven more days until the Kings!" We told our friends about it, and we insisted they pretend to be excited for us. We sang their songs. *"You know that I could use somebody."*

Finally, the day arrived. DawnCheré had carefully crafted and curated the evening. She took me to our favorite Mexican restaurant for a pre-concert dinner date. We had decided to skip the opening act, and she had everything timed perfectly so we could go straight from our romantic dinner to the arena, just in time for the headliner.

Dinner was magical. We laughed and enjoyed each other's company over tacos, salsa, and chips. When 8:00 p.m. rolled around, we knew we had to get going to make it on time. On the drive to the venue, we blasted Kings of Leon songs on the stereo and sang every lyric at the top of our lungs. We were flirting with each other. There was so much love in the air. This was going to be the most amazing evening ever. Our expectations had reached epic heights as we exited the freeway and approached the parking lot at the Bank Atlantic Center.

To our surprise, the parking lot was deserted. My first thought was, *Wow, I thought this band had a bigger following than this.*

DawnCheré said, "I think something's wrong."

"No, this is going to be great!" I'm not one to give up easily. "Let's park the car and go in."

We got out of the car and walked all the way up to the Bank Atlantic Center doors, and our fears were confirmed. Nobody was there. The lobby was abandoned, the doors were locked, and the lights were off.

So I said, "Babe, let me see those tickets."

DawnCheré was all full of attitude. "I know what they say. Concert at 7:30 p.m. at the Bank Atlantic Center."

"Girl, just let me look at the tickets."

She handed me the tickets, and I read them. And then I nearly yelled, "These don't say Bank *Atlantic* Center. They say Bank *United* Center! We're in Fort Lauderdale, and the concert is in Coral Gables. That's an hour away! We'll never make it in time."

DawnCheré started to cry. "This is the worst surprise ever," she whispered. "I ruined everything."

I replied, "Quit crying! You can't cry on my birthday. This is my party." Actually, I didn't say that. I'm not that insensitive. I told her how much I appreciated her efforts, and I think I lied about loving her surprises. Obviously we missed the concert that night. We still haven't seen the band live. But at least it was a memorable night—just for all the wrong reasons. We ended up laughing and making a memory out of it. To this day it's one of our favorite stories to tell other couples.

Have you ever missed the message in the something? Have you ever overlooked the main point? Bank Atlantic Center . . . Bank United Center. They sound so similar, yet they are so different. For DawnCheré and me, missing the message only resulted in missing a concert. But when it comes to following Jesus, the consequences are much more significant.

Jesus came to earth with a specific message. His teachings, his miracles, his reactions to people, and his death and resurrection all communicate one main point. Yet it's far too easy to miss it. This can happen to the best of us—and probably has. Even well-intentioned, good-hearted, and spiritually minded people can overlook it. We might have a portion of the message; we might have a version of the message; but we miss the main theme.

The problem is if we miss his message long enough, we'll end up somewhere God never intended us to be, and we won't like the result. I find many people are spiritually confused and worn out, not because Christianity is hard or God is a tyrant, but because they have missed what Jesus came to say.

Some people think Jesus came to preach about good works. They think the goal of his life was to get us to talk better, act better, *be* better. Following Jesus, therefore, is about behavioral change. It's about fixing yourself and those around you, not necessarily in that order.

Others think Jesus came to establish a holier-than-thou country club religion. His goal was that a bunch of abnormally self-disciplined (and equally self-righteous) people would get together, call themselves the church, and spend their days dispensing judgment against a sinful world.

Still others think Jesus was merely a philosopher. He was a good man, an inspiring teacher. He didn't deserve what happened to him. "Too bad he ticked off the establishment," they say sadly. "It always happens. Only the good die young."

Some think Jesus' life was a protest against evil. His martyrdom was his message. His life and death were a legacy and an inspiration, but nothing more. The list of opinions goes on. Some people say he was a rebel, a zealot who wanted to overthrow the Roman empire and failed. Some say he was an apocalyptic prophet who believed and preached the end of the world was imminent. Others say he was insane, or a con man, or a liar.

The more I read the stories about Jesus and listen to his words, the more convinced I am that those views and others like them fall short. Jesus didn't come simply for behavior modification. He didn't come to create a religious club or clique. He didn't come merely as a philosopher or martyr or life coach. Jesus' message is far more simple, yet far more powerful, than any of those concepts.

Exploring who Jesus is and why he came is the central question of this book. I don't want to miss what Jesus came to say, and I'm sure you don't either. If he is who he said he is—and he said he is God—then it's only logical we make sure we get his message straight. What was he trying to tell us when he spent three and a half years roaming a tiny country in the Middle East? Why did he heal people? Forgive people? Call people to follow him? Why did he die and rise again? And based on all that, how should we live our lives today, two thousand years later?

Maybe you aren't too sure about Jesus' claim to be God. In your mind, the jury is still out on whether his words and teachings should carry weight in your life. That's okay. That doesn't bother me a bit. We are all on a journey of getting to know God, life, and ourselves. None of us has all the answers, least of all me. But even if you aren't sure where you stand on Jesus or the Bible, most of us would agree that for some reason, Jesus lived a uniquely impacting life.

For some reason, his birth split human chronology in half.

For some reason, his teachings and his story resonate in the human heart.

For some reason, millions of people, from every nation, in every century, attribute positive changes in their lives to him.

For some reason, people pray in his name, and time and time again, report answers to their prayers.

For some reason, his teachings and principles are so integrated into our thinking that we often quote him and don't even know it.

So, what was his message? And whom is it for? The answer might surprise you. And it may impact your life forever.

Jesus and the Gangster

To answer the question, I want to look at a little story in the gospel of Matthew. The Gospels—Matthew, Mark, Luke, and John—are full of stories meant to paint a picture of Jesus. They present in gritty, compelling detail a man consumed with a message.

One of the most revealing stories is how Matthew, a man formerly known as Levi, encountered Jesus. This brief story reveals much about Jesus' message and mission.

Before I jump into the story, you might be wondering why this guy had two names. One of my favorite movies growing up was called *Three Ninjas*. The plotline revolved around three kids whose grandfather was a ninja. He trained them and gave them ninja names. Samuel, Jeffrey, and Michael became Rocky, Colt, and Tum Tum. I'm not sure why the last one got such a lame name, but those kids were amazing. They could beat up grown adults. I always wanted a ninja name.

Matthew was clearly not a ninja. But his occupation did

require a non-Hebrew name. He had been born Levi, a Jew. At some point, however, he became known by a Greek name, Matthew. His name and his identity, just like the Three Ninjas, were inextricably intertwined. There was an important reason for that, which I'll get to in a bit.

Later in life, Matthew turned out to be an incredible guy. He was one of Jesus' twelve disciples and one of the authors of the New Testament. He wrote the gospel that bears his name, which is why most of us remember him.

Much earlier, though, before he met Jesus, he was not a nice person. Actually, that's an understatement. Matthew was the quintessential bad guy. He wasn't just run-of-the-mill bad—he was an outright criminal. He was blatantly and intentionally and famously bad. He was the kind of person parents warned their kids about and crossed the street to avoid.

Before he met Jesus, Matthew was a tax collector. Now, you probably didn't gasp or blush when you read that, but anyone living in that day and culture would have. Back then, a tax collector wasn't the robe-wearing equivalent of an IRS employee. He was more like a mafia boss, a gangster. Matthew the tax collector was not a man to be trifled with. He put the "original" in OG. He was like all three *Godfather* movies in one person.

At the time Rome was the supreme world superpower, and Israel was one of the lands they had conquered. The Roman army was notoriously brutal and barbaric. Numerous historical accounts record Rome sacking cities. They would often kill many of the men, rape the women, and enslave the children. History recounts instances when the army lined the streets with people dying on crosses so anyone who entered would know the force and power of the Roman kingdom.

9

After conquering a new territory, the Roman government would impose taxes on the local subjects. That's where Matthew came in. His job was to collect taxes from his own people to give to Rome. In other words, he betrayed his people for a paycheck. And here's the kicker: tax collectors were required to turn in a certain amount of money to Rome, but they could keep anything they collected above that. They were allowed—even expected—to extort money from their own people to line their pockets. They were traitors, thieves, and bullies. It's no wonder they were hated so fiercely by their own people.

This was the reason Matthew went by his Greek name. Greek was the language of the day, so Levi would not have been the most culturally acceptable name to the Romans. Matthew had been born into the nation of Israel, God's chosen people— but he didn't care about that. He cared about money, power, and notoriety. So instead of being Levi the Jew, he took on a new identity: Matthew the tax collector. Matthew the traitor. Matthew the extortionist. By working for Rome, Matthew had turned his back on his Jewish heritage.

To put this in context, imagine that a foreign power has attacked your country. First they kill, rape, imprison, or enslave your family and friends. Then they begin to rule your life with an iron fist. To top it off, they impose a suffocating tax; and to collect the tax, they hire your neighbor. Suddenly the guy you used to grill steaks with in your backyard is your enemy. Now he uses everything he knows about you against you. With the full backing of the conquering nation, he takes what he wants from you and your loved ones. Eventually you can hardly feed your kids, and he has a Ferrari parked in his driveway.

You tell me. Is that a good person? Is that someone you

want to hang with? Is that someone you are excited about going to church with? Is that someone you would trust with anything you value?

Me neither. That's why it's so startling that Jesus made friends with people like Matthew. He didn't just talk to them; he loved them, he called them, he changed them, and he made them part of his story. It's unbelievable.

Here's how Matthew himself described his encounter with Jesus. Like a true godfather, he referred to himself in third person:

> As Jesus was walking along, he saw a man named Matthew sitting at his tax collector's booth. "Follow me and be my disciple," Jesus said to him. So Matthew got up and followed him.
>
> Later, Matthew invited Jesus and his disciples to his home as dinner guests, along with many tax collectors and other disreputable sinners. But when the Pharisees saw this, they asked his disciples, "Why does your teacher eat with such scum?"
>
> When Jesus heard this, he said, "Healthy people don't need a doctor—sick people do." Then he added, "Now go and learn the meaning of this Scripture: 'I want you to show mercy, not offer sacrifices.' For I have come to call not those who think they are righteous, but those who know they are sinners."
>
> (MATTHEW 9:9–13 NLT)

Notice that Jesus didn't give Matthew an application to fill out. He didn't put him on probation for three months. He didn't make him pinky promise to never extort money again.

He didn't even lead him in the sinner's prayer. Jesus simply said, "Follow me and be my disciple" (verse 9 NLT).

Really, Jesus? people must have been thinking. *What qualifies this gangster to be your disciple?* In their minds, being Jewish was the only chance for salvation. Matthew the wannabe Roman was a textbook sinner, the epitome of evil, a prime example of people the Messiah would one day come to judge.

Yet Jesus called him. And Matthew followed. Just like that.

We read it so quickly and casually sometimes, but when you stop to consider who this man was, the implications are staggering. Just look at the reactions of people back then. "Why does your teacher eat with such scum?" they asked (verse 11 NLT). That's probably the sanitized, PG-rated version of what they actually said.

Today, if a celebrity or high-profile person talks about Jesus, there is often instant pushback from religious people. "What could he know about Jesus? Have you seen his music videos? Plus, he's on his third marriage! And everyone knows he does drugs. He can't possibly know God." Often they even quote Bible verses that appear to back up their judgmental stance—verses about fruit, about holiness, and usually about hell.

I am certainly not contradicting those verses. And I understand the need for holiness. My full-time job is helping people understand how to apply the Bible to their lives, after all, so the existence of sin is job security. I'm kidding—but my point is serious. If we truly want to follow Jesus, then we have to understand his message and his heart.

Jesus sought out and befriended a known criminal. Then he named him one of his core group of followers. If that doesn't fit in our paradigm, then we need a new paradigm.

The Message

Let's be honest. Sometimes we make it too difficult for people to follow Jesus. We forget faith is a journey, and on that journey we all are in different places. We can't expect that a person who is just beginning to follow Jesus will have the faith, actions, or vocabulary of someone who has been in relationship with Jesus for years. God certainly doesn't.

A while back someone came up to me at church after I finished preaching. He had recently started attending, and he was clearly excited about what he had heard that night. He loudly exclaimed, "That was f-ing amazing, man! I f-ing love your preaching!" Except he didn't censor himself.

It was the best compliment ever. I loved it. My favorite part was that he didn't realize what he was doing. Why should he? He didn't know you don't typically use the F-word in church. All he knew was that God was real and he was changing his world.

Religion tends to look for outward signs that we are qualified to follow God, but Jesus shatters that paradigm time and time again. He doesn't wait for us to clean ourselves up or renounce our lifestyles. He finds us where we are and calls us to follow him. No application or qualifications needed. That's why I think Matthew's story is such a perfect illustration of Jesus' message.

So, what was Jesus' message? It wasn't that good

> He doesn't wait for us to clean ourselves up or renounce our lifestyles. He finds us where we are and calls us to follow him.

13

people go to heaven. It wasn't that bad people will be judged. Those are cheap imitations of his message.

Jesus' message was *grace*. It was salvation for all who believe in him. It was mercy and compassion and forgiveness for all who would put their faith in him. And I'll go even further. Jesus was the personification and the embodiment of grace. In other words, Jesus *himself* is the message. Jesus is the purpose and the point. The message isn't mere dogma or doctrine. It isn't behavioral change. The message is that no matter who you are or how badly you've messed up, grace and forgiveness are available in Jesus.

That's why Jesus came to earth in physical, tangible, human form. He came not only to tell us *about* grace, but to literally *be* grace for over thirty-three years. His life was his message, and his message gives life. The more we follow Jesus, the more we find our lives defined and transformed by God's love and grace.

Jesus' life is the message of grace. It's a message of unconditional and unending acceptance by God, based on his grace and received through faith in Jesus. I've discovered that it's one thing to agree with grace or even recite verses about grace, but it's another to truly understand it and live it. Honestly, that's where we tend to miss the message the most. We listen to grace on Sunday and then live with guilt, law, and condemnation Monday through Saturday.

Who Jesus is and why he came to earth is the best news the world has ever heard. It's not hard news, bad news, complicated news, or frightening news. It's *good* news. The message of Jesus is one of hope, joy, peace, and freedom.

When Jesus is our message, we realize that everyone is a candidate to be called by God. Rather than being stuck on people's current behavior, we recognize we all are equally qualified—or better said, equally *un*qualified—to be followers and disciples.

Matthew understood this about Jesus. When he threw a party for Jesus, the guest list consisted of "many tax collectors and other disreputable sinners" (verse 29 NLT). This was not the typical squad of a Jewish teacher. I can imagine Matthew calling all his friends: "You've got to meet this Jesus guy. He accepted me. He believed in me. He loved me. He delivered me. He changed me." He wanted them all to meet Jesus.

Christians often ask me how I am able to be friends with certain people who don't adhere to their definition of a Christian lifestyle. "It's simple," I usually reply. "Because Jesus was."

Some of them get it. But some of them counter, a bit defensively, "Sure, Jesus hung out with people, but only to save them. They repented and followed him."

"Not true," I'll say. "Many did. But many didn't. When it comes to faith, everyone is on their own journey. But they still need friends along the way."

In Matthew's narrative, we don't read that the guests had to sit through a sermon to meet Jesus. All we see is that they had dinner and drinks together. We don't know what he said, but we do know that he sought them out, he spent time with them, and he developed a relationship with them.

We tend to measure out our love based on what we'll get back. We will spend time with people and love them as long as there is hope they'll change. Not Jesus. He didn't write off anyone. He didn't consider it a waste of time to invest in people who might never respond. Friendship wasn't a means to an end, but an end in itself.

Has it ever occurred to you that since Jesus is God, he knew who would ultimately reject him or receive him? He healed hands that would hurt people. He restored feet that would run back into sin. He opened eyes that would lust. Why? Because Jesus loves everyone. He loves deeply and unconditionally. Jesus stays consistent even when we are inconsistent. He loves even when we hate. He is faithful even when we are faithless.

The Jesus message is not one of religion but of relationship. Jesus goes to the party, not to let the party get into him, but to get into the party because he loved the partiers. He went to show God's love to people who might not want it or believe it or accept it—at least for now. Ultimately, who is the judge of what is "worth it"? Not us, that's for sure. Only God knows what is happening in people's hearts.

Finding the Pharisee Within

It is very difficult for religious people to be friends of sinners, because religion seeks to control, to impress, and to conform. Religion apart from relationship is more concerned about outward behavior than inward change. It values performance and perfection.

The Pharisees were the standard of holiness in Jesus' day. They were also, at least in general, arrogant and mean. Instead of showing mercy and leading people to God, they condemned and discouraged people. Jesus regularly called them out for their judgmental attitudes, usually using terms like "blind fools," "snakes," and "hypocrites" (Matthew 23:16–33). No wonder they weren't fans.

The crazy thing is, they didn't mean to be that way. They

thought they were pleasing God. They were working hard to eradicate sin in themselves and in the people around them. Unfortunately, they were missing the message of Jesus entirely.

The Pharisees were frustrated with Jesus because he was supposed to be a rabbi, yet he hung out with heathens. Criminals, really. They thought the point was to avoid sin, but Jesus had a habit of seeking out sinners. So they started asking the question, "Why are you a friend to such terrible, awful sinners?"

Jesus' answer was brilliant, but it is often misinterpreted. He replied, "It is not the healthy who need a doctor, but the sick. . . . I have not come to call the righteous, but sinners."

If you've been around church for a while, you've probably heard this quote. It's recorded in the other gospels as well. I think most people would agree that this is a noble, compassionate, altruistic sentiment. My guess is even the Pharisees appreciated it. I think it appeased their concerns. They probably said to themselves, *Oh, that makes sense. He's trying to help those poor, misguided souls. He wants to show them their wrongs so they can turn their behavior around. He's just like us: a good person helping bad people be better.*

But they missed the point completely. And honestly, we often do too. Apart from Jesus, there is no such thing as a "good person." There is no distinction between righteous people and unrighteous people, or between healthy people and sick people. Without the grace of Jesus, there is only one category: sinner. Sick. Unrighteous. Dead, to be exact.

Jesus was trying to communicate his message, but many people missed it. He was saying that he came to save everyone, but only those who recognize their need for salvation will be saved.

I can picture these Pharisees walking away satisfied with his answer, maybe even more arrogant than when they came. They probably felt justified in their self-proclaimed goodness, confident they were in a separate category from "sick" and "sinners."

When we miss the Jesus message, we become blinded by our good works, religion, and self-effort. We think there are areas in our lives that are righteous apart from grace. The gospel of Jesus doesn't lead to arrogance of self—it leads to acquiescence to Jesus. It leads to humility and to dependence on God.

It's so easy to judge the Pharisees. They seem like fictitious Disney characters to us. I always imagine Jafar from *Aladdin* every time I read the word *Pharisee*. And yet, from time to time, I think there is a Pharisee inside each of us. I know there is in me. I recognize his selfish ways whenever I think I am better than someone, when I compare my sin to someone else's sin, when I think my morality impresses God, or when I think my struggle isn't as dirty to God as another person's struggle.

Whenever I think I am any different from Levi the tax collector, I am in danger of missing the Jesus message. His message isn't a political message. It isn't a social justice message. It isn't an economic message. It isn't a gender rights message. It isn't an environmental message. The Jesus message is that we are all born sick, but Jesus came to heal us. We are sinners, but he came to call us to repentance. In him there is grace, there is wholeness, and there is life.

> **The Jesus message is that we are all born sick, but Jesus came to heal us.**

The apostle Paul described a visit he made to the Corinthian church this way: "I didn't try to impress you with polished speeches and the latest philosophy. I deliberately kept it plain and simple: first Jesus and who he is; then Jesus and what he did—Jesus crucified" (1 Corinthians 2:1 THE MESSAGE). In other words, everything Paul had preached to them could be summed up in Jesus and his work on the cross. That is what matters; that is all that is needed.

When it comes to following Jesus—especially in the context of church and other people who are also Christians—it's so easy to mix our message. Why? Because for humans, grace is not the default. We have to learn how to live that way. Our default mode is Pharisee. It's to rate, rank, and judge people based on outward actions.

Grace levels the playing field, though. Grace reminds us that we are all equally bad. We are all tax collectors, so to speak. But here's the good news: *we are all friends of Jesus.* If he's the friend of sinners, and if we are sinners, then he is our friend. Not because we earned it. Not because we even asked for it. But because God loves the world, and he sent his son, Jesus, to save the world.

Outward actions and changed lifestyles are important. Sin hurts us, after all. It robs us of our humanity and strips us of our dignity. We were created to live better than that.

Holiness, however, is the result of salvation, not the road to it. Better behavior is a byproduct of the work of Jesus—and not even the most important one. Love, peace, joy, freedom, and other internal transformations are far more significant than dropping fewer F-bombs or kicking a cocaine habit. But when we miss the message, we start to think actions and behavior are the goal.

We can't afford to get wrapped up in the effects. We can't

get the order reversed. We must be consumed with the cause and the goal of life itself—Jesus. Getting ourselves or others to do things for Jesus is never the goal. The goal is knowing Jesus. It is putting our faith in what he did for us on the cross. It is returning to God, the Creator of our souls, and finding our home in him.

When we meet Jesus, of course, we will experience genuine life change. Matthew left everything to follow Jesus. This is what happens with the gospel. The reasonable response to a true encounter with Jesus is inner and outer transformation. Your priorities change. Your values change. Your social circles change.

Even though meeting Jesus results in massive life change, the emphasis is not on how hard we must work to accomplish that change. The emphasis is on Jesus. When we follow him, we find ourselves taking steps and making decisions we probably never would have dared to attempt on our own.

I can think back to a couple of times in my teenage years when I had clear, personal encounters with Jesus. I knew he was real, I knew he was speaking to me, and I knew I wanted to respond. Those were life-altering moments. I remember praying passionately, "Jesus, take all of me. Where you call me, I will go. Everything I have is yours. Ask me anything Jesus . . . I am yours!" It's easy to pray those prayers as a teenager because you don't have much to lose. Even spending your life on the mission field in Africa seems like an upgrade from sharing a room with your younger brother. The older we get, though, the more cautious we tend to be.

Not so with the message of Jesus. It creates a boldness like nothing else. Matthew the tax collector had never been to church or seminary, but he had one encounter with Jesus and immediately left his lifestyle behind and charged full speed toward the things of God. Following Jesus doesn't lead to safer living. It leads to risk, sacrifice, and change—yet it's the most satisfying life imaginable.

When we value friendship with Jesus first, rather than behavior, and when we recognize that he is our friend because he wants to be, not because we deserve it, everything changes. That is the

> When we recognize that he is our friend because he wants to be, not because we deserve it, everything changes.

power of understanding the message of Jesus. We will find ourselves growing and changing from the inside out. Suddenly, life looks different.

Depression is no match for our joy.

Addictions are not our identities.

Temptations can be overcome.

Sin holds no power.

Victory is within reach.

The future is full of potential.

Who would you be in Matthew's story? Saint or sinner? Pharisee or friend? Holier than thou or wholly messed up? Regardless of who you are or what you've done, the heart of God is the same: he loves you. Right now, right here, just as you are.

Like Matthew, Jesus is your friend. He is calling you to know him, to rest in him, and to follow him. Will you let him?

CHAPTER 2

MORE THAN PANTS

FOR A NUMBER OF YEARS AFTER GET-ting married, DawnChoré and I were not able to have children, which is a journey we've been very public about. However, God has truly done a miracle, and we are beyond thrilled to welcome a baby boy into our family very soon. Now that we are expecting, our friends think they have to mentally prepare us by telling us horror stories about their own small children—but despite that, we are very excited about the future.

Since we didn't have kids of our own for so long, though, I am thirty-plus years old and still know very little about them. All our friends have kids and babies, and I'm the awkward guy. I'm nervous to even hold a baby. It's so much responsibility.

I ran into a friend of mine the other day who is a new mother. She had her baby with her, and I said, "She's so cute! How old is she?"

She replied, "Thank you! She's twenty-two months."

I stared blankly. She might as well have told me her baby's weight in tons or her height in parsecs. It meant nothing to me.

I'm sure parents out there would have nodded knowingly and started dispensing advice appropriate for a twenty-two-month-old. Not me. I just started calculating how many months old I am and wondering at what point it's socially acceptable to drop the months and round to the nearest year.

The worst problem with my lack of parenting experience is that I assume if a kid can hold any level of conversation, then he is basically a miniature but fully functioning adult. If a child can verbalize my name, I take it for granted he can cook, clean, and clothe himself.

A few years ago my mom's extended family met in Hawaii for a family reunion. On my mom's side of the family I have fourteen cousins. Most of them are in their thirties, married with children, so tiny humans were underfoot everywhere. In total there were forty-three of us. It was the best kind of pandemonium imaginable. For seven days we invaded Maui like a wrecking ball. From the beach to the pool to luaus to late-night dinners with the ones we love the most, the week was jam-packed with memories.

The adults were put on a rotating schedule for babysitting duty. That included me, which I didn't mind because I like to think of myself as the fun uncle, the slightly crazy uncle. And I was going to make sure those kids knew it. Hero uncle, that was me.

On my first shift I took some of them to the playground. I had about ten second cousins or nieces and nephews—or whatever they are—around me when a lady walked by handing out popsicles. She asked us if we wanted some.

I said, "We absolutely want popsicles!"

We savored our treats as we walked back toward the pool.

The off-duty parents were relaxing until one of the moms saw us and said, "Rich, where did you get the popsicles?"

I answered innocently, "I don't know, some random lady gave them to us."

"Rich!" my cousin scolded me. "You can't teach the children to take things from strangers." I guess I forgot that rule.

Honestly, I can see myself being the first babysitter in the history of humanity to get kidnapped *with* the kids. An old rickety van would pull up, and some sketchy guy would say, "Hey, I can't find my kitten. Wanna help?"

And I would say passionately, "Guys, come on! We've got to find this cat. Get in the van!"

That would be me.

Near the end of our trip, I was on pool duty, pretending to be a lifeguard for a bunch of four- and five-year-old hooligans. To say they were getting the best of me would be an understatement. In particular, my four-year-old second cousin, Levi, was terrorizing me. He was making noises and pushing me, trying to get me to respond.

I kind of growled a little, "Chill, dog." I was thirty, and he was four, but that's how I talk. I'm not sure he understood. At that age it's hard to tell if the mania is from demon possession or too much sugar. He certainly didn't chill. He didn't stop. I kept saying, "Hey, for real, man, stop. Seriously, knock it off." I even did the "I'm going to count to three" thing my mom used to do.

My patience and diplomacy got me nowhere, though, and finally I had had enough. I grabbed him and threw him in the pool. I didn't plan to do that. I didn't think about it, obviously. I just did it. The kid needed to learn.

His mom was sitting next to me. She has two other kids,

so Levi is a third child. You can always tell the parents of third children. They are so chill. She didn't even move from her comfortable chair. She just said, "Rich, he doesn't know how to swim."

"What?" I yelled. Immediately I jumped in the water to rescue him. I felt like Mitch Buchannon from *Baywatch*. I grabbed him and pulled him out of the water. He had a look of terror mixed with hatred on his face. He was never in any real danger, but he didn't know that. He just knew the guy who was supposed to be watching out for him had tossed him into the pool, and he was furious with me. So much for hero-uncle status.

Have you ever met someone who doesn't know how to apologize correctly? Yeah, that would be me. I mumbled, "Hey, bro, I'm sorry, but, you know, you deserved that. You shouldn't have been messing with me." The poor kid is going to be scarred forever. Eventually he forgave me, and it turns out I am his favorite babysitter. I think it was a bonding moment.

In retrospect, the crisis occurred because I overestimated his skills. I thought because he could talk well, he could swim well. And he thought because I looked like an adult, I was responsible and wise. Turns out we were both wrong.

It's a simple illustration of how easy it is to overestimate people. Sometimes we assume something about someone only to discover, often too late, how different reality is from our expectations. We end up feeling disappointed, desperate, and emotionally depleted.

Here's the problem. When we are let down, we often decide to play it safer next time. We fear disappointment, so we simply lower the bar and expect less. We assume people will let us down. Rather than overestimate them, we subconsciously determine to *underestimate* them. The pendulum of trust swings to the other side because it's safer that way, or so we think.

Maybe it's a faithful wife whose husband walked out on her. Or a hardworking dad whose son ran away to chase an addiction. Or a daughter who never met her parents because she was abandoned at childbirth. Or an employee who was thrown under the bus by a boss for something that wasn't his fault. The list goes on and on. When we feel betrayed and let down, a common response is, "Next time I won't hope for as much."

Cynicism toward those around us is bad enough—but many times we project our earthly hurts onto our heavenly Father. I know I'm guilty of doing this, and maybe you are too. Because people have failed us, we think God might fail us too. So we hold back a bit of trust. We retain some control. We play it safe because we don't want to get hurt again.

Sometimes we underestimate the message of Jesus. We underestimate who Jesus is and how powerful and perfect his grace is. We think we have to help grace out a bit, that we have to do our part. And in so doing, we can end up undermining what Jesus came to do.

After all, we set the bar low because we don't want our hopes crushed and our dreams shattered. But could we ever have such a high opinion of Jesus' character and his power that the reality would disappoint us? I know we feel like God has let us down sometimes, especially in moments of tragedy or disappointment. Those emotions are real, and we all have experienced them. But ultimately, when our lives are over and our stories are told, will we look back and be disappointed in God? Will the reality of who Jesus is and what he has done let us down? Or will we wish we had believed more, dreamed bigger, and worried a little less?

Underestimating Jesus' message might ultimately be worse than missing his message. We can think we understand God and know all about the gospel, when actually we've settled for a life far short of what God designed for us. Then we wonder why it's not working for us, and eventually we might decide the whole following Jesus thing just isn't for us.

> **We can think we understand God and know all about the gospel, when actually we've settled for a life far short of what God designed for us.**

God knows our human tendency to withdraw and withhold. But rather than taking offense at our small view of him, he took the initiative to change it by sending Jesus.

The Problem with Good

In Mark chapter 10, Jesus tells the story of the rich young ruler, a man who sorely underestimated Jesus and his message of grace.

> As Jesus started on his way, a man ran up to him and fell on his knees before him. "Good teacher," he asked, "what must I do to inherit eternal life?"
>
> "Why do you call me good?" Jesus answered. "No one is good—except God alone. You know the commandments: 'You shall not murder, you shall not commit adultery, you shall not steal, you shall not give false testimony, you shall not defraud, honor your father and mother.'"

"Teacher," he declared, "all these I have kept since I was a boy."

Jesus looked at him and loved him. "One thing you lack," he said. "Go, sell everything you have and give to the poor, and you will have treasure in heaven. Then come, follow me."

At this the man's face fell. He went away sad, because he had great wealth.

(VERSES 17–22)

Here was a guy who in everyone's eyes had everything: youth, wealth, power. Most people would declare him a success. Yet he still felt like he was missing something. He had questions he couldn't seem to answer. His story reminds me of that famous U2 song:

But I still haven't found what I'm looking for.

Over the years I've had the opportunity to meet many people from many walks of life. I've discovered the people who appear to have it made are often the ones living in the greatest torment. You can accumulate stuff, you can be successful, you can be famous, you can be rich—yet if you haven't addressed the condition of your soul, you can still be miserable.

Some people live their whole lives seduced by success. Always climbing, always winding and grinding their way forward, but always missing the beauty that's around them. They think a moment of true contentment will come; however, for many of them, that moment never comes. Why? Because contentment is not found in a vacation home, Instagram followers, or a seven-figure job. You can't build a life on money, fame, and power. They are as fickle as the wind.

Sometimes we underestimate Jesus because we overestimate

ourselves. But eventually, if we are honest, we realize we aren't enough. Something is missing. I think that's where this man was. Despite his outward success, he had nagging doubts. *Am I enough? Am I good? What do I still need to do?* He approached Jesus and said, "Good teacher, what must I do to inherit eternal life?" (verse 17).

Immediately we notice something: his approach was completely off. That matters a lot, by the way, because the way we approach people indicates how we view them. For example, I speak to my wife differently than I speak to my buddies. You probably talk to your boss differently than you talk to your kids. Approach reveals perception. Approach reveals value. Approach reveals whether we underestimate, overestimate, or properly estimate the qualities and capabilities of the person we are approaching.

The problem here was that the young man, in his opening line, called Jesus *good*. Jesus instantly called him out for it. "'Why do you call me good?' Jesus answered. 'No one is good—except God alone'" (verse 18). I read that passage and wonder, *What's so important about the word* good? Why did Jesus jump down the guy's throat as if he had made a mistake?

After a decade of marriage, I've discovered something: *good* can mean different things to different people. For example, it means something very different to men than it does to women. It all depends on how you say it. If you are a single male, I'm helping you out here. This could save your life.

Let me illustrate. My wife likes me to accompany her when she is shopping. She's shopping for herself, mind you, not for me. But she wants me to be there. I think it's because she likes my company, or it might be because she wants me to pay for everything. Sometimes I wonder.

We'll go into a department store to buy a pair of jeans. She has to try on nineteen pairs of jeans in order to buy one, and I sit in that weird chair that's usually situated just outside the dressing room while she's inside. It often gets awkward because dressing rooms are almost always located in the middle of the women's underwear section. I feel like I have to assure anyone who walks by, "It's okay—I know someone in there. I promise."

Then my wife will walk out to show me a pair of jeans. She's barefoot, but she always stands on her tiptoes likes she's wearing heels, and she's excited. "Babe, babe, babe—I love these! How do they look?"

Again, this is awkward. Men don't do this. We don't do mini fashion shows in front of other dudes and ask, "Bro, bro, bro—how do these jeans look on me?"

When she asks me how she looks, I usually reply, "Babe, you look *good*. Those jeans look good on you." Why? Because to a man, good means . . . *good*. *Good* is a good word. Very versatile. "You look good, girl. So good."

But no! *Good* doesn't mean good to girls. It means average. Mediocre. It means, "You think I look fat in these jeans." If I like the jeans, my wife wants me to lose my ever-loving mind. She wants enthusiasm, colorful adjectives, and dramatic facial expressions. When she tiptoes out and says, "Babe, babe, babe—how do these look?" I need to reply, "Wow! Sweet Jesus! There is a God, and he loves me! Those are amazing, girl! Oh, oh, oh! Buy four pair. Buy five pair. You better buy all they've got, because you are next level gorgeous in those jeans!"

"Really, you like them?"

"Absolutely! I love them."

"Mm . . . I'm not sure, actually. I think I'll try on eighteen more."

Back to the chair.

The reason DawnCheré objects to the word *good* is because it is an understatement. It is safe, noncommittal, generic. It's the easy way out.

That was exactly why Jesus objected to it. This young ruler had underestimated Jesus. He had heard rumors that he was the Messiah, the coming Savior, God in the flesh—but he wasn't ready to go that far. He wasn't prepared to admit that the man in front of him was actually God and, therefore, the ruler of his life. So he played it safe. "Good teacher . . ."

Notice that Jesus' reply wasn't motivated by an inferiority complex. Verse 21 says, "Jesus looked at him and loved him." In other words, Jesus corrected him for his own good. He saw the man's heart, and he knew he needed a clearer picture of who Jesus was, or he would never receive the answers he was looking for. Why? Because how we perceive someone doesn't just dictate how we approach them—it dictates how we *receive* from them.

The rich young ruler didn't see Jesus as God. He didn't see him as Messiah. He didn't see him as Savior. He saw him simply as a good teacher. He was saying, "You are a rabbi. You are a good teacher. So, good teacher, give me some good principles. Give me some life lessons, some advice. Help me settle my soul. Help me find peace."

Rabbis were highly educated, intelligent, incredible men who had given their lives to understanding the Torah, which was God's law. They had memorized the first five books of the Bible. Most of us, when we try to read through the Bible, never make it past the book of Leviticus. These guys knew the entire thing by heart. They were serious about obeying God and keeping his requirements. They were constantly answering questions, giving advice, and interpreting the Scriptures. They were good people.

But here's what was wrong with the way the man was describing Jesus. Jesus is a teacher, and Jesus is good. But he is so much more than that. He is *God*. That was what he was gently reminding this young man.

Some people read this and say, "Look, Jesus says right there he is not God."

No, he is saying the opposite. He is saying, "Only God is truly good. So if you call me good, you are equating me with God. Are you prepared for that? Are you willing to see me as God? Not just a rabbi, teacher, counselor—but God? And if I am God, address me the right way."

Sometimes people tell me, "I believe in God, but I'm not sure about Jesus. I think Jesus was a good guy. I think Jesus was an amazing teacher. But I don't believe he was God."

You can't have it both ways. The only way for Jesus to be a good teacher is for him to be the Son of God and the Savior of the world. C. S. Lewis, one of the great Christian apologists, famously said that Jesus is either a liar, a lunatic, or Lord.[1] Why? Because he claimed to be God. He claimed to have come to earth to save humanity from their sins. Merely "good" people don't talk that way. Only crazy people or diabolical liars say things like that—unless you really are God.

Let me put it this way. If someone walks up to you and tells you he is Zeus incarnate and you should bow before him, how would you react? First, you'd assume he is crazy. You'd back away slowly. You would avoid running into him ever again. But then, if you somehow determine the guy isn't insane, the alternative is even worse. He must be intentionally leading people astray. He's a liar. A deceiver. A cult leader trying to take advantage of people for his own gain. So the dude is either a lunatic or a liar, but by no stretch of the imagination could he be called good.

The same holds true for Jesus. If you don't think he was insane, and if you don't think he was deceiving people, then there is only one option left. He is Lord. He is God. He is the Messiah and Savior he claimed to be.

Many people want Jesus to be part of their lives, but they don't want him to be Lord of their lives. It doesn't work that way. Jesus is not a shout-out at an awards speech. He is not a good luck charm. He is not a piece of jewelry. As it has often been said, either Jesus is Lord of all or he is not Lord at all.

The Wrong Question

The rich young ruler's approach wasn't the only thing that was wrong. Take a look at his question: "What must I do to inherit eternal life?" The question isn't evil—but it's the wrong question entirely.

I hear the same thing all the time in our culture and society. People are fixated on the concept of what they have to *do*. "How do I make it to heaven? How do I find peace? Am I good enough? Have I done enough? What steps must I take to be good, to live well, to please God, to be fulfilled?"

This is especially true for people who are successful. Often they attribute their success to themselves. They are used to working hard and getting the job done. They assume eternal life is achieved the same way. "Hey, Jesus, I've got a problem. Tell me what I must do to solve it."

When the young ruler asked what he had to do to inherit eternal life, Jesus responded with the traditional rabbinical checklist: "You must not murder. You must not commit adultery. You must not steal. You must not testify falsely. You must not cheat anyone. Honor your father and mother" (verse 19 NLT). It was exactly what the man expected from merely a "good teacher."

These things were part of God's law, which was the ultimate authority for these ancient Hebrews. God had given his law—his rules, his requirements, his expectations—to Moses thousands of years earlier. *Law*, therefore, was more of a religious term than a legal one. It was a synonym for keeping God's requirements for holiness. In Jesus' day, Israel defined themselves as a people and evaluated themselves as individuals based on the law.

The young man must have smiled smugly and thought, *Great! Been there, done that. I've been following that list since I was a kid. I'm good. I knew I was, but I was just checking in. Just wanted to make sure.* Notice what religion does. Religion makes you proud of yourself and your efforts. The gospel makes you proud of Jesus. The man started to leave. "Thanks, Jesus. You're such a good teacher. I'll be on my way now."

Jesus wasn't done, though. "Oh, before you go. Just one more thing. Sell all your stuff and give away the money. Then come, follow me."

Then come some of the saddest words in Scripture: "At this the man's face fell. He went away sad, because he had great wealth" (verse 22).

Wait, what just happened? Why did Jesus keep pushing the man to do more until finally the man just gave up?

It's crucial that we understand what went on in this scenario. The point wasn't that money is evil. Money was just the straw that broke the camel's back. It was the tipping point.

The point of this story is the man thought Jesus was simply there to help him be good. He reduced Jesus' message to a self-help program. Talk about an understatement! Jesus didn't come to earth to help good people get better. He came to bring spiritually dead people back to life. None of us are good—only God is good. That's what Jesus said. If the young man had really known who Jesus was, he would have fallen to his knees and cried, "Lord, save me!" But he asked for rules, laws, checklists. He asked for medicine instead of a miracle.

Jesus knew exactly what was going on in this man's heart. So he gave him law. And more law. And even more law. Until finally, the poor guy gave up.

That's what the law does, by the way. It never stops making demands. It's a burden we cannot carry. It's a constant reminder that we aren't good enough, holy enough, disciplined enough, perfect enough. By *law*, I'm not just talking about the ceremonies, rituals, and rules in the book of Leviticus—I'm talking about the moral obligations and righteous requirements implicit in being human. We might not all agree on what those are, but we do agree on the majority. Don't lie, don't steal, don't murder, don't lust, love people, be generous, be patient, forgive, serve, work hard . . . the list is just as long as it has ever been. And just as impossible to keep.

At my age I'm starting to have a love/hate relationship with my mirror and my scale. Why? Because they tell me the truth.

In my mind, I'm a cross between David Beckham and Brad Pitt. But then I look in the mirror and see wrinkles I didn't think I had. I look at the scale and realize I should probably hit the gym more.

The law is a moral mirror, a spiritual scale. It tells us the truth. When we look at God's commands, we realize we aren't as faultless as we thought. We see God's perfection, and that highlights our imperfections.

The most important part, though, is that the law was not given to drive us to despair, condemnation, or self-works. It was not designed to make us walk away sadly, like this young man. The law is meant to drive us to Jesus. But until we admit we can't be good enough on our own, we won't look to Jesus for anything more than pats on the back and helpful life suggestions.

If we approach Jesus simply as a teacher, he will give us the law. But if we approach him as our Savior, he will give us grace. The rich young ruler should have said, "Jesus, I don't think I can do that. I guess I'm not as selfless and disciplined as I thought. I need grace. I need forgiveness. I need you."

The law is full of demands, but grace is full of supply. That is why Jesus said, "Do not think that I have come to abolish the Law or the Prophets; I have not come to abolish them but to fulfill them" (Mathew 5:17). Why would Jesus fulfill the law? Because even on our best day, we couldn't.

The great tragedy of our generation is not that people don't think about Jesus. It's that they don't think highly enough of him. I am convinced that it's impossible to overestimate

> **The law is full of demands, but grace is full of supply.**

Jesus. But most of us, including myself, have been guilty of underestimating him.

When we underestimate Jesus, it usually has nothing to do with whether we think he can heal or provide for us. We don't underestimate his power. We underestimate his grace. We think—just like the rich young ruler—that he came to make us better. Jesus is not a self-help message. Jesus is a "he did all the work because you couldn't" message.

Was this man guilty of greed? Of course he was. Jesus went on to talk about that later in the chapter. But let's be honest. So am I. So are you. Thankfully, our weaknesses are not recorded in the Bible, but we all have them. Is the answer to go home, clear out our bank accounts, and give everything to charity? Does that make us fit to follow Jesus? No! There will always be one more area to fix, one more good deed to do.

Greed was not the young man's greatest error. His greatest error was that he underestimated who Jesus was. He reduced Jesus to his tiny box, his narrow paradigm, his cute little checklist. How many times do you and I do that? How many times do we underestimate Jesus' sufficiency? His mercy? His wisdom? His power? How many times do we reduce this message, this good news, to a self-help program? To a lesson on morality? Jesus didn't come for behavior modification. He came for a heart transformation.

He's Bigger Than That

My mother used to tell me about a missionary in the denomination she grew up in, a man named Charles Greenaway. In the

1950s, Charles took the gospel into some of the most remote areas of the African Congo. Many of the tribespeople wore little clothing, if any. Think *National Geographic*. Charles dedicated his life to preaching Jesus to these tribes, and he had astounding success.

On one occasion some minister friends were visiting from America. When Sunday rolled around, men from the village attended the church service in their typical Sunday attire: which was essentially nothing on bottom, or at least not enough to cover the bare essentials, in the minds of the visitors.

The guests were appalled. In righteous indignation, they approached Charles after the service. "Charles, this is not right. This is embarrassing. How can you let these men worship like that? Why don't you make them wear pants?"

Charles's answer was as simple as it was profound, "Because I don't want Jesus reduced to a pair of pants."

I don't know if the visitors got his point, but that story has stayed in my mind for years. Jesus did not come so people would wear pants. Duh. Of course. How ridiculous would it be to reduce the gospel to a change of wardrobe?

Yet we do the same thing when we believe or preach that the message of Jesus is primarily a message of behavior modification. When we think we can make ourselves more acceptable to God by changing our behavior, we are reducing his message to a pair of pants. When we imply with our sideways glances and passive-aggressive comments that people just need to "fix a few things" in order to be true followers of Jesus, we are reducing his message to a pair of pants.

Jesus is so much bigger than that! Tim Keller, founder of Redeemer Presbyterian church in New York City, said it this way: "If there is a God, you owe him far more than a morally decent life."[2] Jesus did not come to give us good teaching, good doctrine, or good morals. He came to be our Lord and Savior, and he came to give us life.

Yes, our behavior will change as we follow Jesus. But it will never be the result of self-effort or self-condemnation. It will be the result of his grace, love, and power. As we rest in the finished work of our Savior, we will be rescued and changed into his image day by day. It's inevitable. It's glorious. And it's his doing, not ours.

There is no three-step process to get into heaven. There is no formula, no checklist, no instruction manual. There is only a person: Jesus. We can't achieve Jesus; we can only receive Jesus. He is not a supplement; he is the Savior. He is the answer. He is the door to God. He is the one-stop shop for all our questions and concerns.

> **We can't achieve Jesus; we can only receive Jesus.**

Got problems? *Jesus.*
Got addictions? *Jesus.*
Got mistakes? *Jesus.*
Got regrets? *Jesus.*
Got questions? *Jesus.*
Got fears? *Jesus.*

Jesus is bigger than our good deeds or our bad deeds. He came when we didn't love ourselves. He came when we were cursing him. He is more than we have ever dreamed. He is bigger and better than we have ever thought. We can't overestimate him. We can't exaggerate his love.

Our failures fade into oblivion in the face of his amazing grace. Temptation and addiction are no match for his measureless mercy. Guilt is gone. Condemnation cannot make us hang our heads. Shame has been replaced with the quiet confidence of Jesus' love.

I want to be known as a man who continually attempts to overestimate Jesus. I want my life to find hope in the message of Jesus and his scandalous grace. I want my identity to be in him, not in my checklists or accomplishments.

How about you? Have you been guilty of reducing Jesus? Are there areas of your life where you are underestimating him? Maybe it's time to dust off old dreams, to dare to hope again. God is for you. God has a plan for you. God is your Savior and your rescuer.

No matter what you are facing, look to Jesus. Raise your hopes, elevate your opinions, and recalibrate your expectations. You can't overestimate him. You can't think too highly of him. You can't expect too much of him. Jesus is more than enough! Why not put yourself in a position that says, "I am going to try to overestimate Jesus"? Jesus is who he said he is—and who he is will be more than enough for your every need.

CHAPTER 3

WEIGHT SHIFT

I'VE NEVER BEEN VERY GOOD AT WORK-
ing out. I love the *idea* of working out—just not the execution of
it. Maybe you can relate. Or maybe you are one of those insane
people who enjoy pain, sweat, and self-inflicted torture. (If you
are, I'm worried about you. That's not normal. And it makes the
rest of us look bad.)

I remember going to the gym once when I was about twenty
years old. I was minding my own business, doing bicep curls
or something. Out of nowhere, this guy came over. He was a
muscle guy—you probably know the type. He had muscles
coming out of weird places. "Hey!" he said, a little too aggres-
sively. "You're doing this all wrong!"

I thought, *Nobody asked you.* There was no way I was going
to say that to this dude, though.

Then he asked, "How old are you? Fourteen? Fifteen?"

"Um, seventeen," I totally lied.

He growled, "We are going to do this workout together." He
sat on the bench behind me and wrapped his arms around me

from the back. Then he started moving my arms up and down until I achieved the proper form. The entire time I was thinking, *This is not happening. Rich, just try to find a happy place.*

When we finished, he said, "I'm going to be in here every day this week. Let's do this again."

I thought, *Thank you for the warning. I'm never coming back here.*

In retrospect, I don't think I've ever recovered from that day. The whole gym experience is just too much for me.

There are people at the gym—I'm not making this up; I've seen them—who like to *run for fun.* I can't imagine what that must feel like. My vision of hell would be an infinite line of treadmills where people run in place for eternity. When I run I usually end up making this weird breathing noise, and I convince myself I have asthma. I think technically it's called being "out of breath," but since I don't usually get to that stage, when it happens, I immediately assume I'm going to die.

Yes, I go to the gym, but not because I want to. I go because I have to. I go because my wife makes me go. To be honest, the gym has taught me some invaluable lessons. My first experience with hot yoga taught me never to wear long pants in hot yoga. My first time at spin class reminded me girls are never to be underestimated. (I still see that instructor in my nightmares.) My first and only attempt at CrossFit confirmed I look silly with my shirt off. Those are good life lessons.

The most priceless truth I've learned, however, is this: carrying weight that is too heavy can injure you. I have firsthand experience with this, and on multiple occasions.

If you hate working out, you are probably wondering, *why would you lift weights that are too heavy?* It's simple. I have a big ego and small muscles, and that's a dangerous combination. More times than I'd like to admit, I've attempted to lift too much. And in most of those instances, I end up pulling a muscle or pinching a nerve in my neck. Then I walk around like C-3PO from *Star Wars* for a month. At least it's an excuse to avoid the gym for a while.

The results of carrying too much physical weight are easy to see: injury, pain, fatigue, limited mobility, frustration. We can also carry too much weight on a soul level, and the negative effects on our souls are far more significant than a pinched nerve. How many of us carry—on an ongoing basis—emotional, spiritual, or mental burdens beyond our abilities? What effect might that have on our emotions? Our relationships? Our thoughts, reactions, and decisions?

Jesus told the people who came to hear him speak, "Come to me, all of you who are weary and carry heavy burdens, and I will give you rest. Take my yoke upon you. Let me teach you, because I am humble and gentle at heart, and you will find rest for your souls. For my yoke is easy to bear, and the burden I give you is light" (Matthew 11:28–30 NLT). In other words, God wants to carry the weight that is too heavy for us, and he does that through Jesus.

In my previous book, *Sandcastle Kings*, I talked about the weight of the law: the rules and standards we as humans falsely think we should keep. I looked at how Jesus came to carry that burden and give us rest. He accomplished what we could never accomplish on our own, and now he calls us to find rest in him.

A lot of people never come to know Jesus as the friend of sinners, and as a result, they live with a figurative stiff neck.

There have certainly been times in my journey with Jesus when I've felt this way, and maybe you have too. We can find ourselves worn out, in pain, and limited, not because God is asking too much of us, but because we are insisting on carrying too much. Instead of letting Jesus carry our weights by his grace, we are often convinced we have to do it ourselves.

God knows all about our oversize egos and undersize strength. He is far more understanding and far less condemning than most people give him credit for. King David said it this way: "The LORD is like a father to his children, tender and compassionate to those who fear him. For he knows how weak we are; he remembers we are only dust" (Psalm 103:13–14 NLT).

Jesus is the friend of sinners. That means he has an ongoing relationship with us; he is continually committed to our well-being.

It seems a lot of times we are okay with Jesus saving us, but we think we have to sustain ourselves without him. "Thanks for saving me, Jesus! I've got it from here!" Then the weight starts to crush us, and we wonder what we're doing wrong.

> The more we come to know Jesus as the friend of sinners, the more we will be able to truly find rest for our souls.

Jesus is not just the Savior—he's the sustainer. He's not just the author of our faith—he's the finisher, the one who perfects and completes and carries our faith through to the end. The more we come to know Jesus as the friend of sinners, the more we will be able to truly find rest for our souls.

Ask yourself, *What unnecessary weight am I carrying today? What burdens have I made my own that God never intended for me?*

Weights We Carry

One of the most common weights I see people carrying is the weight of yesterday's performance. So many individuals are internally bound by the blunders of the past. The message of grace is that your history does not determine your destiny. Your failures do not have to frame your future.

The apostle Paul said, "Forgetting the past and looking forward to what lies ahead, I press on . . ." (Philippians 3:13–14 NLT). Do you know why he said that? Because he had a dark past. He was literally a Christian killer. In the name of God, he imprisoned or slaughtered those who followed the teachings of Jesus. Imagine the level of guilt he faced. Yet, after he encountered Jesus, he let go of the shame and condemnation. Nothing behind him was going to help what was in front of him. To step into the future, he had to forget the past. The same is true for you and me.

Paul also had to let go of his successes. He was a Pharisee, and a highly successful one at that. He listed some of his accomplishments and qualifications a few verses earlier in the passage I just quoted. Then he said this:

> I once thought these things were valuable, but now I consider them worthless because of what Christ has done. Yes, everything else is worthless when compared with the infinite value of knowing Christ Jesus my Lord. For his sake I have

discarded everything else, counting it all as garbage, so that I could gain Christ and become one with him. I no longer count on my own righteousness through obeying the law; rather, I become righteous through faith in Christ. For God's way of making us right with himself depends on faith.

(PHILIPPIANS 3:7–9 NLT)

Past success can be as paralyzing as past failure, because we can end up holding ourselves to some artificial measure of success. We define ourselves by what we have accomplished, and we carry the weight of maintaining that image.

Whether your past holds good things, bad things, or a mix of both, Jesus wants to give rest to your soul. Learn to lean on him and to find your value in him when life's burdens grow too heavy.

Maybe it's not the past that's haunting you; it's the present. Maybe the pressures of today are weighing on your soul.

There is the pressure of *being good enough*. Many of us live with the secret fear that if people discover who we really are, they will reject us. So we hide behind a façade of perfection— and it's exhausting.

There is the pressure of *getting it all done*. We live in a fast-paced world where everything is urgent, everything is important. Stress is normal. Adrenaline is a way of life. To deal with it all, we drink multiple overpriced caffeinated drinks a day, as if pumping caffeine into an already overstimulated brain is going to help.

There is the pressure of *earning God's acceptance*. That shouldn't be a pressure because his love is unconditional. But often we forget that, and we think we have to achieve a state of near perfection before we dare expect God to answer our prayers or bless our lives.

If you find yourself bending and breaking under the stresses of today, there's a story at the beginning of the Bible that might help you out. It's the creation story in the book of Genesis. One thing that has always stood out to me is what God said after every stage of creation. He would look at his work and simply say, "It is good." And he'd move on.

Have you ever considered how much more God could have created? He could have made two earths instead of one. He could have made a butterfly that would wake you up every morning singing your name. He could have made real unicorns, instead of just letting them be something junior high girls dream about. He could have created you with an "undo" function that would let you take back dumb comments after they leave your mouth.

Sometimes you just have to say, "It's finished. It's good. I'm done." You could always do more. That's where the pressure comes from, right? Yet God wants to whisper in your ear at the end of the day, "Good job. I'm proud of you. You did your best, and it was amazing. Now let me do what you could never do." And while you are eating or sleeping or watching Netflix, God accomplishes the impossible on your behalf.

Maybe the past or present isn't weighing you down, but the worry of tomorrow is. What if the economy tanks? What if my boss gets mad? What if the bank forecloses? What if my marriage fails? What if my kids grow up and hate me? What if I'm not good enough, smart enough, rich enough, fast enough, strong enough?

If you stop and think about it, though, most of what we worry about never happens. Worry is a waste of time, energy, and mental health because none of us knows the future. Only God can see beyond this exact instant. So rather than being preoccupied and concerned about what might, possibly, maybe, tentatively happen, we need to learn to rest in the God who doesn't just *know* the future, but who *controls* the future.

Jesus himself commanded us not to worry. "Can any one of you by worrying add a single hour to your life?" (Matthew 6:27). Worry indicates we are trusting in our own plans and schemes more than we are trusting in Jesus. It means we are carrying weight we were not designed to carry, weight that will eventually harm us. Worry can't help us—it can only hurt us. The only thing worry changes is our blood pressure.

Come to Me

Notice the first phrase in Jesus' invitation to experience rest from Matthew 11: "*Come to me.*" The word *come* is a command, which means we must respond. Jesus, the friend of sinners, came to help us all, but we have to come to him. None of us deserves his assistance, yet all of us have access to his grace. Jesus is extending an invitation that is ours for the taking.

Sometimes we don't come to him because we think we are bothering him or we think our need isn't big enough for him. We need to understand the gospel. We can never do it on our own, and we don't have to. That's the beauty of Jesus, the friend of sinners. He came to forgive a debt we could never resolve. He came to pay a price we could never afford. He came to carry what we could never shoulder on our own. No matter what weight you are struggling with, Jesus can take it for you.

DawnChéré and I live in downtown Miami. It seems like every day a new building is going up nearby. Our apartment is surrounded by construction sites with cranes stretching into the sky. The purpose of a crane is simple: to lift heavy objects. For that to be possible, the crane must have a counterweight that weighs more than what is being lifted. It's just physics, but there's a lesson in there for us: Jesus is the counterweight for every sin, every weakness, and every failure.

What Jesus accomplished on the cross weighs more than your sin and shame. He came down to earth so we could rise up to heaven. Jesus can lift any weight because he is bigger, he is more powerful, and he is greater than anything you might face. He's been lifting humanity's burdens for thousands of years.

Remember when Israel was trapped between the Egyptian army and the Red Sea? Moses was helpless. The people were desperate. Then God split the waters, and Israel strolled to safety. Or how about Joshua at the battle of Jericho? I'm sure he and his men were strategizing beforehand, trying to figure it all out. But they couldn't. Then God said, "I have a strategy: just march and watch, and I'll take care of the walls." God's power far outweighed walls and armies. Then there was Gideon. He and three hundred homegrown soldiers faced an army that outnumbered the sand on the seashore. Talk about impossible odds. But in a matter of moments, God brought about victory.

What weight, what burden, what responsibility seems too big for you? Ultimately, the answer isn't to work more, sleep less, try harder, save more, spend less, plan better, or strategize more. None of those things has the power to lift your weight.

The answer is a *person*. Jesus can carry your weight because

Jesus is bigger than your weight. It's not about what you can do—it's about what he already did.

Take My Yoke

The second command in Jesus' invitation in Matthew 11 is "take my yoke upon you" (verse 29 NLT). Sometimes we are good at coming to Jesus, but we usually aren't very good at taking his yoke. But unless we learn what it means to receive his yoke, we will live frustrated, exhausting lives.

It can be hard to understand the metaphor because many of us have never seen a yoke. Yokes are often associated more with third-world agriculture than with our high-tech, city-savvy lifestyles. So when Jesus tells us to take his yoke, we agree it's necessary and spiritual and awesome; but we don't really know what he's talking about.

When some of us hear this verse, we sigh internally in despair. *A yoke? Isn't that an instrument of hard labor? I'm already overburdened. How can I take Jesus' yoke on top of what I'm already carrying?* If that's our reaction, we've missed the metaphor entirely.

A yoke is a wooden instrument placed on two oxen so they can plow a field in tandem. The goal of a yoke is to accomplish more by working together. Jesus is telling us to stop working on our own and instead work with him. His yoke keeps us attached to him. His yoke keeps us in step with him. His yoke keeps us pointed where he is going. His yoke makes our burdens bearable and our journey enjoyable.

Taking his yoke upon us isn't about pulling more weight.

It's about letting him pull our weight. He will carry what we could never carry. When we harness ourselves to him—to his grace, his power, his sufficiency—everything changes. We will accomplish things we never thought possible because we are yoked to the supernatural power of Jesus.

Here's what often happens, though. We pray, we plead, we tell Jesus why we need help, we complain about the weight we are carrying, we ask for answers—and then we stand up, shoulder our burden alone, and walk away, exactly the same as before. "Good talk, Jesus. Thanks for listening. Glad I could get that off my chest. Well, back to the daily grind. Wow, my life is so hard." And off we go, struggling under the same impossible burdens as before.

For Memorial Day a few years ago, DawnChéré and I had some friends over. One of our friends brought her son with her, who is one of my favorite kids in the world. His name is Mkai, and it happened to be his fifth birthday that day. The kid is a legend. He's a heartbreaker already. He's cool, calm, and collected, all at the age of five.

Some other friends pulled up in an SUV stocked with groceries for the party, and we all began unloading the car. I said, "Mkai, want to help carry stuff into the house, man?"

"Yeah!" He was absolutely pumped to help. He ran over and grabbed a big box with me. He couldn't even see over it, but he was convinced he was going to carry that beast inside with me. He even made grunting noises the whole time.

The funny thing was, he wasn't helping at all. All he did was get in the way. He was wiggling, yelling, and laughing the whole time. He thought he was carrying so much weight, but I was doing all the work.

He might not have been much help, but that wasn't the point, was it? I asked him to help because I loved having him there with me. His presence brought me joy, and his exuberance and excitement were what was important to me—not the amount of help he was.

I don't mean to burst your bubble, but Jesus doesn't need you and me to get the job done. Sometimes we take ourselves so seriously, as if the success of the universe depended on our perfect performance. It doesn't. God's got this. He's been doing it for a long time, and he's really good at it.

He *wants* our involvement, though. He loves it. Most of the time we get in the way more than anything else, but he doesn't mind. The point isn't getting work done; the point is relationship. And, ironically, relationship is the key to getting work done. When we work from a place of rest and connectedness, our work is more effective; it's sustainable; it's fulfilling.

Jesus isn't against working hard. That's exactly why he chose the metaphor of a yoke: it implies purpose, direction, and accomplishment. But he wants us to work with him, not on our own. He wants us to live life by his side, connected to him, learning from him, and being led by him.

> We were created to walk together with God, and when we do, we find rest for our souls.

We were created to walk together with God, and when we do, we find rest for our souls. Rest is an internal posture of trust that actually enables us to accomplish more in life, because we are working in tandem with Jesus himself. That's what is so unique about Jesus' message of rest: his yoke brings us rest while it simultaneously brings us greater life satisfaction and productivity than ever before.

Trust Is Scary

There's a little verse in 1 Peter that messes with me every time I read it. You've probably heard it. It's 1 Peter 5:7: "Cast all your anxiety on him because he cares for you." Another version refers to "casting all your care upon Him, because He cares for you" (NKJV).

This verse doesn't just tell you to cast your cares upon God. It tells you why you can cast your cares on him: "because He cares for you." I think this is the key to the whole process. You wouldn't put your trust in someone who doesn't have your best interests in mind. Trust is scary.

Cast my cares on God? we think. *Uh, then what? Who's going to care about my cares if I don't care about them? Sure, God cares a little. It's his job. But does he care about what I care about? And does he care about it as much as I do?*

We have trouble trusting God to do a better job caring for us than we could for ourselves. After all, most of us have been let down by people more than once in our lives. We've learned to look out for number one. But God is not like us. He is not like the authority figures who have betrayed us. He is not like the friends who let us down.

You can trust God because he cares for you. And if he cares for you, then he cares about what you care about even more than you do. He cares if the doctor's report comes back positive. He cares if the bills get paid. He cares if you've gone through a breakup. He cares if your marriage is on the rocks. He cares about the pornography addiction. He cares about the bankruptcy. He cares about the lawsuit. He cares that you didn't get the job you wanted. He cares about the fender bender, about the mortgage, about the bullying at school. God cares about it all because he cares about you.

Are you convinced that God cares for you? Until you are convinced, you will never cast your cares on him. You will carry on alone, caring and carrying too much.

God has been caring for you since the very beginning. How has God shown his care for you? Think about it for a moment.

He cared for you when he knit you together in your mother's womb.

He cared for you when he put a purpose and a destiny in you.

He cared for you when he came to earth to redeem humanity.

He cared for you when he showed himself the friend of sinners.

He cared for you when he was accused falsely, tried unjustly, and sentenced to death.

He cared for you when he was stripped naked so you could be clothed in righteousness.

He cared for you when they put a cross on his back and marched him to Calvary hill.

He cared for you when they laid him on his back and drove six-inch nails through his hands and feet.

He cared for you when he looked out at the sea of people and said, "Father, forgive them, because they don't know what they are doing."

He cared for you when he bore your sin, the biggest and most impossible burden you could ever have.

He cared for you when he was resurrected the third day, declaring to all humanity this was the death of death.

He cared for you when he promised to be with you until the end of time.

I could go on forever, because his care goes on forever. You will never find the end of it. His love won't run out. His affection knows no end. You can't exhaust his mercy, exasperate his patience, or escape his compassion. And because he cares for you, you can cast all your cares upon him.

Cast Your Cares

Many of us have heard that we are supposed to cast our cares upon God, but we sometimes wonder if this verse really means what it says. Casting our worries on God sounds a bit like escapism, like denying reality. It sounds irresponsible.

Some even think helping Jesus out is more spiritual than casting their cares on him. Letting Jesus carry the load—they think—is for the weak, the immature, the desperate. Somehow worrying and stressing out make them feel like they are carrying at least part of the load. Others assume Jesus only cares about the big problems in life. And since he's running the universe, their daily doubts and petty problems aren't worth his time.

But none of that is true. We don't need to do life in our strength! We don't need to carry our share, to help God out, to buck up and shut up and carry on alone. We are called and commanded to cast our cares on him.

"Casting" takes effort, by the way. It takes intentionality. Sometimes we say things like, "Let go and let God," but casting is more than that. You can't inadvertently cast a heavy pack onto someone else's back. You can't accidently cast a fishing line. Casting is a decision, and it's yours to make. Will you cast your cares upon God? Or will you complain to him, ask for his help—and then walk away with the weight still on your shoulders?

When I turned twenty-nine, my wife got me the strangest gift ever. It was a watch. *What's so strange about a watch?* you might be wondering. Well, this watch is unique. It doesn't tell time. It doesn't have gears or a battery or hands or even numbers—it's just a wristband with a blank face. It's a watch that's not a watch.

I tried to act excited. "Wow, it's a wat . . . bracelet. It's incredible! It's beautiful! What a concept. A watch that doesn't tell time. I've always wanted that, babe! Thank you!" I'm a great actor.

My wife said, "Rich, this is not just any watch. This is called an Infinity Piece. And there's a meaning behind it."

"And what is that?" I said. But really I was thinking, *First the Kings of Leon concert, now a watch that doesn't tell time—no wonder surprises aren't my thing.*

"Well, I got you this watch that doesn't tell time because time is irrelevant when you are doing what you love." She kept going. "Rich, what I love about you is you do what you love, you love what you do, and you live the moment you are in to the fullest."

"Dang, girl, you can make anything sound good!" I said. "What time is it? Time to make out?"

Whenever I wear my watch, people either love it or hate it. I was in New York eating at a restaurant, and the waitress saw it. "Oh my goodness, I love that watch!" Then she noticed it didn't have hands or numbers. "So, what time is it?"

I started into my speech. "I don't really know what time it is, and it doesn't matter because time is irrelevant when you're doing what you love."

"That is so stupid," she snapped.

I was a bit taken aback. I thought, *Thanks a lot, Debbie Downer. Who asked you?* I kept a straight face, though. Like I said, I'm a good actor.

She wasn't done sharing her uninvited opinion. "That watch is for people who don't have any real responsibilities."

I thought, *Ouch. That hurt my feelings a little bit.*

And yet, that is what 1 Peter 5:7 is like to so many people. "Oh, that verse is so cute. Cast all your cares upon Jesus. That's a nice verse, but it's for people who don't have any real responsibilities. It's for people who don't have actual pressure and worry. It's for people who don't have a past like my past. That verse works for some people, but not for me because I live in reality."

That is dead wrong. If you feel like you are carrying so much weight that you can't take another step; if you feel like you've injured yourself emotionally and mentally because you've borne too much for too long; if you feel like life is overwhelming and you're facing it alone—then you are precisely the person Peter was writing to. This verse is for you.

On the other hand, if you are twenty-eight years old, sleeping in your parents' basement, and playing video games all day, you probably don't need this verse. Your mom says, "Honey, you should get a job." And you say, "I don't need a job, Mom—I'm casting my cares on Jesus." No, you're not. You're casting them on your mom. Get a job, get some responsibilities, and then you'll understand how important this verse is.

This verse is for the single mom who wonders, *How will we make it? I can't juggle work and kids and schools and schedules. I can't do this alone. It's too much.*

It's for the teenager who thinks, *Yeah, but Dad left. He said he would be here, but he walked out on us. We are broken. We are hurting. God, can you really carry this?*

It's for the college student who lies awake worrying about the future. *Is there a place for me in this world? Will I find a spouse? Will I find a job? Student loans, the economy, the environment, terrorism, wars—I'm overwhelmed.*

It's for the parents who mourn together, *What about our son who left home? Where is he? What is he doing? Where did we go wrong? We can't fix his addictions; we can't break through to his heart.*

This verse is for you. It's for me. It's for real people, living in a real world, facing real problems, and carrying real responsibilities. Cast your cares on him. That's what he is there for. That's what he does.

Make a Weight Shift

A few years ago DawnChéré and I had the opportunity to go to England while I completed a study abroad course. One weekend a group of us went mountain climbing in the Lake District. It was more of a hike, really, but mountain climbing sounds more extreme. There were about twenty-five of us in the group, people of all ages and abilities, plus our guide.

This guide was no joke. He was prepared for the worst, and something told me he was hoping it would happen. From his equipment to his clothing to his demeanor, the man was a true professional.

We started our ascent, and he pushed us hard. He kept yelling, "We stay together. We finish together."

Halfway through the climb, there was one young woman who kept falling to the back of the pack. Time and time again, our guide scaled back and walked with her, all the while encouraging her not to give in. Finally, she came to a breaking point. She was too exhausted and discouraged to keep going.

The guide went over to her. "Are you okay?"

"No," she said, in tears. "This is too much for me. I can't do it."

The guide replied, "I know you can do this. You can make it to the top."

"No," she insisted. "I can't make it one more step."

"I know you can make it to the top, we just have to make a weight shift."

"What are you talking about?" she said.

"Give me your backpack."

The fatigued young woman said, "But then you'll be carrying two packs. It's too much weight."

The guide looked at her and laughed. "Trust me. I've done this before." Then he grabbed her pack and almost jogged to the front of the line. We all made it to the top that day.

I've never forgotten his words: "We just have to make a weight shift." I think Jesus, the guide of our lives, is saying the same thing to you and me. "You can do this. You can stay the course. You can finish the race. Just make a weight shift."

> If you are tired,
> if you are weary,
> if you are ready
> to quit, come
> to Jesus.

What weights are holding you back? What burdens are you bearing that you were never designed for? It's time to make a weight shift. It's time to transfer your cares and concerns and anxieties to the only one capable of handling them.

If you are tired, if you are weary, if you are ready to quit, come to Jesus. Take his yoke upon you. Learn from him. Rest in him. Cast your cares upon him. Trust in his ability to carry you through. Listen for the confident, compassionate voice of your Savior and guide: "Trust me, I've done this before. I'll carry your weight, and I'll get you to the top. Friend, let's make a weight shift."

CHAPTER 4

FAST PASS

BACK IN MIDDLE SCHOOL, LINE CUTTING was an art. Remember those days? We hated it when other people cut in line, but we all did it ourselves. Line cutting was just one of those things that made middle school memorable and slightly traumatic. For example, remember the "chat-and-cut" technique? A buddy would come up to you in line and start a conversation. Casually you would pull him into line with you, and within seconds the merge would be complete, unnoticed and unbegrudged by those behind you.

If the line-cutter wasn't quite as close of a friend, you might give him a "back skip." That's where you let him cut in line, but he had to go behind you. This one often made the person who had been right behind you a bit mad, but he or she couldn't do much about it because it was two against one.

And then, of course, there was the old-school "bully cut." Someone would simply jump in front of you, daring you to do something about it. This technique was usually reserved for kids further along in puberty or higher up the popularity food chain.

Calling them out would result in physical or social harm, so you just kept quiet.

Line cutting was a way of life in middle school, but, unfortunately, some people never outgrew it. I have a tough time with those people. I'm not going to lie. I have been a Christian for a lot of years, but God is still working on my patience, and line-cutters are proof he has a lot of work left to do.

Have you ever had a grown adult cut in front of you? It's six in the morning, and you are in line at the coffee shop. You might be half asleep and barely functioning, but then someone tries to slip in front of you, and instantly you are a viper: alert, venomous, ready to strike. "Whoa. Whoa! Where do you think you're going? The line starts back *there*, buddy."

I tend to make a scene when somebody cuts in front of me in line. My wife can sense it coming. She'll say, "Babe . . . ," which is meant to be a warning. I usually ignore it.

"No, this isn't right," I'll mutter and fume. "He can't do that."

Then I'll glare at the offender and say, "Excuse me, sir. We've been waiting here for a long time. You'll have to wait your turn like the rest of us." If that doesn't work, I'll get the crowd on my side. Public shaming is an awesome thing. "Hey, everyone, this man's a cutter. Right? Come on! Let's stone him!"

I'm that guy. Pray for me.

Why does it bother us so much when someone cuts in front of us? Notice how I just included you in my weakness. It makes me feel better.

I know exactly why. Because it's not *fair*. We waited our turn. We paid our dues. We earned our spot at the front. Now some joker is going to waltz in and act like he belongs there? Not on our watch.

If we can be honest for a moment, the reality is this: we

want people to get what they deserve. We might say we don't, but deep inside we often do. "You did this, so you get that. You didn't do this, so you don't get that."

We aren't quite so justice-minded when it comes to ourselves, of course. We like to be on the receiving end of mercy. We love to be the exceptions to the rule. But when it comes to others, we are going to make sure justice prevails.

That kind of vigilante thinking is bad enough when it comes to line jumpers. But it's far worse when it creeps into our theology and our faith. Why? Because grace isn't fair. The gospel isn't fair. At least not in the way we define fairness. Just look at the story of Zacchaeus.

First Impressions

I love the story of Zacchaeus because it completely messes with our moral assumptions and our petty ideas of justice. The story is found in Luke 19:1–10.

> Jesus entered Jericho and was passing through. A man was there by the name of Zacchaeus; he was a chief tax collector and was wealthy. He wanted to see who Jesus was, but because he was short he could not see over the crowd. So he ran ahead and climbed a sycamore-fig tree to see him, since Jesus was coming that way.
>
> When Jesus reached the spot, he looked up and said to him, "Zacchaeus, come down immediately. I must stay at your house today." So he came down at once and welcomed him gladly.

All the people saw this and began to mutter, "He has gone to be the guest of a sinner."

But Zacchaeus stood up and said to the Lord, "Look, Lord! Here and now I give half of my possessions to the poor, and if I have cheated anybody out of anything, I will pay back four times the amount."

Jesus said to him, "Today salvation has come to this house, because this man, too, is a son of Abraham. For the Son of Man came to seek and to save the lost."

If you grew up in a Christian church, you might remember the Sunday school song about Zacchaeus: "Zacchaeus was a wee little man, a wee little man was he. He climbed up in a sycamore tree, to see what he could see . . ." It had a catchy tune. But I'm not sure it fully captures the scandalous nature of this story.

Zacchaeus wasn't just a short guy. That wasn't his defining characteristic. He was a really *bad* short guy. He was a thief, a crook, an extortionist. We should probably have been singing, "Zacchaeus was a total jerk, a total jerk was he."

Like Matthew, Zacchaeus was a tax collector. He had betrayed his own people to work for the Roman oppressors. But Zacchaeus wasn't your average tax collector. Luke wrote that he was a "chief tax collector" (Luke 19:2). In other words, he was the boss, and he oversaw a gang of mobsters. Luke also pointed out that he was extremely rich. Why is that important? Because Zacchaeus had gained his wealth by extorting from his fellow Jews. So when I read this, I don't like this guy, right from the start. He was not a nice person. He was not a deserving person.

Of course, we've read the end of the story. We know Zacchaeus has a change of heart. We know he turns from being the crooked Sheriff of Nottingham into noble Robin Hood, giving money to the poor.

But the people lining the streets didn't know that was going to happen. All they knew was this was an evil man, and he of all people did not deserve Jesus' attention.

Determined to See Jesus

When you understand how far this man was from being an upstanding, respectable citizen, verse 3 becomes even more shocking. It says, "He wanted to see who Jesus was."

Think about that for a moment. He *wanted* to see Jesus. Something inside yearned to know God, to find peace for his soul. On the outside, he was probably jaded, calloused, and cold. He had everything money could buy. He had reached the pinnacle of his career. But on the inside, he was empty.

Then he heard about Jesus, about his miracles and teachings, and his heart jumped. *Maybe this man has answers. Maybe this man can bring me peace.* So he decided to check him out. He decided to see Jesus for himself. That's where his height issues came into play because he couldn't see over the crowd.

I wonder how many people around us secretly desire to see Jesus. We can't read people's hearts. We can't hear their thoughts. All we see are actions, and actions only tell part of the story. Sometimes we are so quick to judge people's readiness to receive Jesus—and we can be dead wrong.

"That guy? He'll never go to church. He hates church. Hates Christians. Doesn't believe in God. He's a lost cause."

"Do you see her? Her life's crazy, and she doesn't even care.

She's proud of it. She likes it. There's no way she wants to know about Jesus."

I think a lot of people in our lives and in our spheres of influence deeply desire to know God. They might not know what they are looking for. They might have a bad attitude toward the church or toward Christians. Their actions and vocabulary might seem like they are far from Jesus. But inside, they are ready to do anything to see him.

I've discovered it's not hard to show people Jesus—we just have to get out of the way. Zacchaeus couldn't see Jesus because there were a lot of good, upstanding people lining the road, and he was too short. I think there's a message in there for us. Sometimes we are those tall, good-looking, self-righteous people who block the view of Jesus for those who need him most.

I'm going to be blunt right now because this is deeply important to me. Often we think our job is to judge people's actions and hearts, to tell people if they are going to heaven or hell, to convince them they are wrong and we are right and they'd better change, or else.

Really, though, we just need to get out of the way. Often they already want to see Jesus, but instead of welcoming them and drawing them close, we exclude them. They feel spiritually short, they feel inferior, they feel hopeless because we give the impression people only get to see Jesus if they somehow deserve it.

Our role is not to stand tall and proud, to act like we have it all together, to close ranks and keep out sinners. We don't have it all together anyway. We *all* need Jesus. We all fall short of his glory and his standards. What gets in the way of hurting, haunted people who want to see Jesus? Self-righteousness and self-centeredness. What reveals Jesus? A posture of humility and camaraderie.

People will see Jesus in us and through us and because of us. They will see him in our love and in our humility. They will see him in our welcoming arms and warm embrace. They will see him when we show mercy instead of dispensing judgment. They will see him when we reveal our own flaws and scars rather than pretending we are perfect. They will see Jesus in our lives without us saying a word because his light, mercy, and grace shine through us naturally.

> What reveals Jesus? A posture of humility and camaraderie.

Lose It for Jesus

Zacchaeus was so desperate to see Jesus he did two shocking things. First, verse 4 says, "He ran ahead." Why is that such a big deal? Because in Middle Eastern culture two thousand years ago, it was undignified for men to run, especially wealthy, important men. Running was humiliating and degrading. Running was an indication that the thing being pursued was more important than the person running. It was a sign of desperation.

That's why the story of the prodigal son is so scandalous, by the way—the father *ran* to greet his son. The father represents God, and the son represents broken humanity. The parable illustrates how passionate God is to restore us to himself.

Can you imagine a businessman in a three-piece Armani

suit sprinting down the street? It would be anything but dignified. It would definitely make you stop and stare. *What is so important?* you would wonder. *Why is this respectable, successful man running?* The fact that Zacchaeus would run in front of crowds of people shows how desperate he was to meet Jesus.

It gets even crazier. What if that Armani-clad businessman stopped at a tree, dropped his briefcase, and clambered into the branches like some schoolboy? You'd assume he was either out of his mind or fleeing from a pit bull. Yet that's exactly what Zacchaeus did. Verse 4 continues, "And climbed a sycamore-fig tree." He left his moneybags and his scrolls and his dignity on the ground and climbed a tree.

This is crazy. Zacchaeus had totally lost any bit of cool he had. His swag tank was on empty.

It's interesting to note some of the things that make people lose their cool. For instance, some people freak out when they see someone famous. I was in the airport a while back and saw a crowd of people clustered around someone. It turned out it was the actor William Shatner.

The guy sitting next to me didn't recognize him. "Who is that?" he asked me.

"That's William Shatner," I said.

"William Shatner?" he replied. "Hmm. Never heard of him. Why are people going so crazy? It's dumb."

"He's Captain Kirk from the original *Star Trek*," I told him.

Instantly the guy went from condescending critic to fawning fanboy. "You're kidding me! Captain Kirk? Wow! Where's my camera? I have to get a photo!" Two minutes earlier he was oblivious, indifferent, and aloof. Then he found out a celebrity was nearby, and he started acting like a junior high girl at a

Justin Bieber concert. People lose their cool when they see someone famous.

People also lose their cool when they fall in love. Being in
love and being cool are mutually exclusive. Have you ever been
talking to a dude when his girlfriend calls? His voice instantly
changes. When he was talking with the guys, it was normal:
"Bro, you should've see me in that game, dog. I killed it. I was
unstoppable." Then he answers the phone, and he totally loses
his bravado. His voice gets all sweet and croony. "Ah, babe,
yeah, I really miss you too. Can't wait to see you. No, I'm not
doing anything important. Just talking to you, girl. That's all
that matters."

My wife stripped all my cool. I'll never forget when I pro-
posed. It's a fact: you can't be in love and keep your cool. I was
stuttering like you wouldn't believe the whole night. I drank at
least ten cups of water at dinner.

Here's another one. I remember years ago, at college, I saw a
couple across the street. The girl must have had to go to class, so
the guy kissed her good-bye and then started crossing the cross-
walk going the other way. He was totally cool, waving good-bye.
Suddenly a car rolled through the stop sign and hit him. He
rolled off the car and fell to the ground. The crazy part was that
he immediately stood up and tried to walk it off, like nothing
had happened. He waved to his girlfriend. "I'm good! See you
later."

I yelled, "Bro, stop! You just got hit by a car!" I couldn't
believe it. The guy was trying to maintain his image in front of
his girl, but everyone who saw it happen was freaking out. You
can't get hit by a car and keep your cool.

Let me tell you something else. You can't come to Jesus and

keep your cool. You don't come to Jesus swagged out. You don't come to Jesus strutting. You don't come to Jesus with your cool self. You come to Jesus broken. You come to Jesus desperate. You come to Jesus saying, "I'll do whatever it takes just to get a glimpse of who Jesus is."

That is where Zacchaeus was. He had come to the end of himself, and he knew he needed something more. He had to have been wondering, *Is this really worth it? Can Jesus really make a difference? I want so badly to see him. I'm trying so hard to see him. Will he even care?*

Zacchaeus didn't know it at the time, but his effort to see Jesus couldn't compare with what Jesus was going to do for Zacchaeus. Zacchaeus climbed a tree for Jesus, but Jesus died on a cross for Zacchaeus. Zacchaeus did whatever it took to see Jesus, but Jesus did whatever it took to *save* Zacchaeus.

No matter what you've done to reach God, God has done more. No matter how much you want God, God wants you more. Anything you are willing to do for Jesus, he has already done for you. The very fact you desire God is an indication he already desires you and has made a way to be reconciled. God has loved you and known you since before the foundation of the world. Since before you were born. Since before you even cared about seeking him. Long ago he set in motion his plan to save you, forgive you, heal you, and restore you.

> **The very fact you desire God is an indication he already desires you and has made a way to be reconciled.**

He Knows Your Name

Notice that all Zacchaeus did was climb a tree. He didn't say anything. He didn't call out to Jesus. He didn't answer an altar call. He didn't confess he was a terrible person. He didn't promise to change. He just wanted to see Jesus, and that simple fact was enough to stop God in his tracks.

Remember, Jesus was the celebrity in this scene. He had people pulling at him, talking to him, crowding around him, asking for his autograph. Yet he was instantly aware of Zacchaeus, and he held up an entire parade to meet his need. He looked up in the tree and said, "Zacchaeus, come down immediately. I must stay at your house today" (verse 5). Of all the people Jesus could have called out, he chose the least deserving guy—and he called him by name.

Sometimes we think we are on our own in a quest for an elusive God. We assume we've already disappointed God so much we have to beg him for mercy and hope he finds it in his heart to forgive us. Yet Jesus spotted Zacchaeus, perched with pigeons in a fig tree, and rearranged his whole day just to be with him.

God is both big and small at the same time. He's big enough to create the universe and every human soul, yet small enough to know the intimate details of your existence. Jesus called Zacchaeus by name. He knew where he lived. He apparently even knew what was for lunch because he invited himself over. When you're God, you can do stuff like that.

This is the God who wants you know him, to love him, and to be loved by him. A God who can do anything he wants, yet chooses to spend the day with you. The Bible says he knows the number of hairs on your head. All your days were planned out and written out before one of them came to be. He knows when you leave and when you return, when you go to bed and when you wake up. Everywhere you go, he is there. God knows you like no other, and he loves you like no other. Regardless of what you did or didn't do, regardless of your past or your pedigree, if Jesus wants you, he's going to get you.

Every criminal has a story. Jesus doesn't care about the crime; he cares about the criminal. Every sinner has a name. Jesus doesn't care about the sin—he already took care of it on the cross. He cares about the sinner.

If Jesus found Zacchaeus up in a tree, he can find you wherever you are today. In a broken marriage or a broken home, he will find you. In sickness, he will find you. In a failed business, he will find you. In addiction, he will find you. In success or failure, in fame or anonymity, in strength or weakness, he will stop under your fig tree and call you by name. That is who he is. That is what he does.

It's not about your actions or merits. It never has been. It's about his grace, his mercy, that rushes to meet you when you show the smallest inclination toward him. Salvation is by God, for God, through God. His love for you far outweighs your faith in him. You didn't find God—God was never lost. You were. I was. And he found us, and he called us, and he'll never let us go.

Front of the Line

In this story, Jesus sounds like a party crasher, and a demanding one at that. "I'm going to your place, Zacchaeus. Hey, could you make sure the salsa for the nachos isn't too spicy? It gives me digestive issues."

I would have thought, *Wow, that's a bit forward.*

But not Zacchaeus. Verse 6 says, "So he came down at once and welcomed him gladly." He couldn't believe his luck. This was the man everyone said had answers. Real answers. Answers for the soul. And he was going to Zacchaeus's house for the day. It was too good to be true. Zacchaeus was overjoyed.

The rest of the onlookers? Not so much. And with good reason, if you think about it. They were good people. They had needs too. They wanted to see Jesus, and they deserved it far more than this tax collector. Zacchaeus? Really? He was a traitor. He was the guy who stole from his own people, who cheated little old ladies, who lived in luxury because he plundered the poor.

It's no wonder verse 7 says, "All the people saw this and began to mutter, 'He has gone to be the guest of a sinner.'" I would be muttering too. Unless I was Zacchaeus. And that's the point of the whole passage.

Grace is most appreciated by those who need it most. Some of us need to spend less time muttering that someone else was shown grace and more time appreciating the fact we were shown grace.

Jesus didn't come for the most deserving. He came for the least deserving. He didn't come for people who have it all together. He came for those whose lives are falling apart, who need him and know it. At the end of the day, none of us have it all together. We all need Jesus. We just don't all recognize it. Sometimes it's easier to criticize than to appreciate. It's easier to look down on others than to look up to a Savior.

On the other hand, sometimes we can get a sinner complex. We know we are undeserving, but we get so fixated on our failures that we can't come down from our little fig tree. Jesus tries to show us grace, and we stiff-arm him in self-imposed condemnation. Rather than listening to the mutterings of people who don't understand grace, we should listen to the voice of Jesus: "I want to be with you, to love you, to help you. I want to go to your house today."

As far as we can tell in the story of Zacchaeus, there was no sermon. No rebuke. No threats. Zacchaeus simply encountered Jesus, and everything changed. Look at the outcome of this consistent, persistent, pursuing grace in the life of Zacchaeus.

He stood up. He quieted the room. Then he said, "Look, Lord! Here and now I give half of my possessions to the poor, and if I have cheated anybody out of anything, I will pay back four times the amount" (verse 8).

Zacchaeus met Jesus, and it prompted something inside of him to say, "Wow, I've been accepted. I've been forgiven. Now I want to give, I want to help, I want to make things right. Not out of legalism, but out of grace."

Jesus responded, "Today salvation has come to this house!" (verse 9). Just FYI, Jesus was talking about himself here. Salvation wasn't an act of generosity. Salvation was a person, and his name was Jesus.

He continued, "Because this man, too, is a son of Abraham." Then Jesus said something that has changed the way I think about him: "For the Son of Man came to seek and to save the lost" (verse 10). Notice those two words: *seek* and *save*.

I have preached for a long time that Jesus came to save the lost. It is the beautiful story of the gospel. The Son of God became the Son of Man so the sons of men could become the sons of God. It's incredible.

But Jesus didn't just come to save the lost—he came to seek the lost. Why is that important? Because it reveals a Savior who walks to the back of the line, finds the least deserving person, and takes him or her straight to the front.

I was at Disney World a while back with my wife, my mother-in-law, and a friend. We got in line for the Big Thunder Mountain ride. Then we saw the wait time sign: it was going to be a ninety-minute wait! A few minutes later, we were inching along, talking about how unbelievable the line was, when suddenly a random stranger came up to us. He said, "I have four Fast Passes that I can't use. Do you want them?" Fast Passes, in case you aren't familiar with the concept, are tickets that let you skip to the front of the line. I said, "There is a God, and he loves me the most."

We took the tickets. We got out of the line we were in and went to the Fast Pass entrance. We didn't cut in front of anybody, we didn't cheat, we didn't bribe the attendant—we just walked straight to the front of the line and got on the ride. It was glorious. And totally undeserved.

I can't think of a clearer illustration of what Jesus did for Zacchaeus. He didn't deserve Jesus' attention—unless it was a public rebuke. He was the last person there who should have had the privilege of hosting the Savior of humanity in his home. Yet in an instant he found himself at the front of the line. It was as unexpected as it was undeserved.

Jesus says the same thing to us as he did to Zacchaeus. Read Revelation 3:20: "Look! I stand at the door and knock. If you hear my voice and open the door, I will come in, and we will share a meal together as friends" (NLT).

I often hear that verse used in reference to people becoming Christians, but it was written to people who had been following Jesus already, some of them for decades. That means it's possible to know about Jesus but never let him into our lives and hearts.

Jesus already took the initiative to seek us out. He has invited himself over for a meal as our friend. He's knocking at the door, in fact. We just need to respond.

That's easier said than done because it contradicts conventional thinking, which says you get what you deserve. That's why people criticized Zacchaeus, and it's why they criticized Jesus for hanging out with Zacchaeus. Self-righteous religion can't understand grace. Sinners will always accept Jesus. Religion will always shun Jesus. Why? Because religion is about doing, but grace is about what is already done. There's a big difference.

Religion says, "Wait a minute—Zacchaeus belongs in the back of the line! He can't skip to the front. I've been waiting forever. Look at me: I'm a good Christian. I haven't missed church in three years. I read my Bible every day. I tithe. I fast and pray. I deserve it. But this guy?"

> Religion is about doing, but grace is about what is already done.

Can I be honest? That mentality is not the gospel. It's the opposite of the gospel. I am so thankful God doesn't give me what I deserve. I am so glad he accepts me by grace, not by the law.

Maybe you find you have been muttering about people who seem to get what they don't deserve. Or maybe you tend to hide in the branches, all too aware that you don't deserve what you desperately want. Wherever you find yourself, Jesus wants you to understand he knows you, he accepts you, he loves you, and he wants to be with you. Just as you are.

Jesus didn't come to give you what you deserve. He came to give you what *he* deserves. He is your "fast pass." His grace is the reason you can have peace with God and with yourself. You can skip the never-ending lines of legalism, self-effort, and dead works when you have Jesus.

He already found you. He already picked you. He already called your name. Now he's standing at the door of your heart, waiting to be your friend. You just have to open the door.

PART 2

CULTURE: GOD'S LOVE
FOR THE WORLD

JESUS DID NOT COME TO MAKE GOOD
people better—he came to make dead people alive. He came
to do what none of us could do for ourselves, which is save us
from sin and restore us to God through his exorbitant message
of grace.

*Jesus is the friend of sinners, and since we are all sinners, we
are all his friends.* It's the greatest lopsided relationship ever. His
message, his heart, and his passion are to restore humanity to
God through himself. We don't deserve it, and we never will.

This brings up an important question: *Why?* Why is Jesus
the friend of sinners? Why would God send Jesus to earth on
behalf of a broken humanity? Was it worth it to give everything
in the hope that some would return his love?

When you understand the greatness and holiness of God,
it's hard to understand why he would be the friend of people like
you and me. I think if I were him, when I saw how messed up
people had become, I'd just start over. I'd go for Humanity 2.0.

But not God. There is something hardwired into his character that would not allow him to give up on us. Jesus demonstrated that when he came to earth and lived among us for thirty-three-plus years. He proved it when he befriended sinners. He proved it when he embraced our culture, our world, and our humanness by becoming one of us.

Let's explore Jesus' unparalleled passion for people everywhere. We're going to look at why he is so committed to being our friend and what that means for our day-to-day lives. And, finally, we'll see how his passion for the world influences our own interactions with the culture and society we live in.

CHAPTER 5

LOST AND FOUND

I FLY A LOT. THAT'S AN UNDERSTATEMENT, actually. I've logged more than 2.5 million air miles in my lifetime. For the sake of perspective, that's like flying around the earth one hundred times, or flying to the moon and back five times. It seems like nearly every week I find myself in another airport, getting on another airplane.

I don't particularly like flying. I do love getting to share about Jesus in different destinations, especially if those destinations have beaches and warm weather. But flying itself is just a necessary evil to get from point A to point B.

The problem with flying isn't so much flying itself—it's the airports. Have you been to an airport lately? Airports are the one place where panic is a normal emotion. If you are happy in an airport, you'll probably get flagged by TSA for acting suspiciously. You are supposed to be hurried, harried, and haggard because that's what airports are all about.

Everyone is frantic. No one slept the night before or had a real breakfast that morning. Kids are crying, and parents look like they'd like to cry. Ticketing agents are stressed to the max. Everywhere you turn, someone is running desperately to catch a flight.

Once you survive the airport with its lines and its stress, its pat-downs and its meltdowns, the airplane itself awaits. This is slightly better because it means you finally get to sit down. It also means you get to meet your seatmates. I'm a social person, so I don't mind meeting strangers. But can we all admit that sitting inches away from a stranger for hours on end is just a little awkward?

You've just met and you are already sharing an armrest, for starters. You can hear each other chew. You learn how they take their coffee. You inform each other when you have to go to the bathroom, for crying out loud. And if the trip is long enough, you'll probably wake up drooling on someone's shoulder. It's bizarre.

Then there is that moment when you strike up a conversation and start asking each other questions. There is one question, one inevitable line of inquiry, that I dread. *What do you do for a living?*

It's not that I'm ashamed of the gospel. I love being a Jesus follower and a pastor. But I always get one of two responses when they find out I'm a pastor. Some people begin to relive past trauma with God or Christianity and get angry with me. I can handle that response. I don't have to defend Jesus—I just have to love people. Jesus can speak for himself.

The second response, though, is much worse. They start to confess every sin they've ever committed. "When I was in seventh grade, I did . . ."

Just stop. I don't want to know. I probably did the same thing in seventh grade.

The other day I was flying in first class. I didn't pay for first class—I was upgraded because I fly a lot, as I already mentioned. I started talking with the lady sitting next to me, and sure enough, the question came up. "What do you do?"

"I'm a pastor."

Her response was not what I expected. She didn't complain about the church. She didn't list her past sins. Instead, she went into attack mode—because of where I was seated in the airplane, of all things.

"Wait, you're a *pastor*?" she said. "And you're flying *first class*? How dare you! You belong in the back. You're wasting money. People's money. God's money. Humph."

I was speechless, a rare occurrence for me, so I ended up agreeing with her. "Yeah, um, you're right. I usually do fly in the back. Right next to the bathrooms. It's just that, you know, frequent flyer miles . . ."

I felt like I needed a defense, an explanation. I wanted her to understand my motives. I'm sure you've felt that way at some point too. People judge our actions but don't see our hearts, and it can be a bit frustrating.

Jesus faced the same thing. People often accused him, criticized him, and attacked him. On many occasions he remained silent. That's often the best response, and one we should probably employ more often. But there were a few instances where he explained his actions, and these give us incredible insight into the mind and motivation of God.

Luke records one of these instances in chapter 15 of his gospel. People were asking Jesus why he hung out with bad people. It's the same question I have, to be honest, whenever I contemplate how holy God is and how, well, *unholy* I am.

> Jesus is in the business of finding and reclaiming that which is lost.

Jesus responded to the questions by giving his defense, his explanation of why a holy Savior would spend so much time befriending bad people. Jesus' defense was simple: *he is obsessed with lost things.* Jesus is in the business of finding and reclaiming that which is lost. Luke 15 illustrates this beautifully.

Obsessed with Lost Things

Here's how Luke set up Jesus' story.

> Tax collectors and other notorious sinners often came to listen to Jesus teach. This made the Pharisees and teachers of religious law complain that he was associating with such sinful people—even eating with them!
>
> So Jesus told them this story.
>
> (LUKE 15:1–3 NLT)

Then Jesus proceeded to tell a parable, or a story, with three parts. Each part was a different metaphor, but all three made the same point. We call the first part the parable of the lost sheep, the second the parable of the lost coin, and the third the parable of the prodigal son. That last title is a misnomer, by the way. I'll get to that in a bit.

These three metaphors in Luke 15 are an amazing window into how Jesus thinks. So often we defend ourselves based on our own ideas, our own convictions, our own feelings, our own callings. But we need to understand the heartbeat of God and allow his defense to be our defense, his motives to be our motives, and his passions to be our passions.

Notice that two distinct groups listened to Jesus that day: sinners and religious leaders. The Pharisees and other religious leaders complained the loudest. "Jesus, you claim to be holy. You are supposed to be an example. Some people even say you are the Messiah, God himself, our Savior. But that's impossible, because you hang out with the wrong crowd. You should be a judge of sinners and a condemner of sinners, but instead you are a friend of sinners. We don't get it."

On the other hand, there were the sinners themselves. They probably didn't get it either. I can imagine them saying, "No one has ever told us about a God like this. No one has ever shown us a love like this. This man seems to be perfect, yet he is our friend. We don't deserve it. We don't understand it. Could God really love us that much?"

So to answer both groups, Jesus told several stories. I love that. Sometimes we make things so complicated. We have our systematic theology and airtight arguments and doctrinal debates, and then Jesus gives us stories. Doctrine and theology are good, of course. Don't get me wrong. But Jesus' love is so simple we can miss it if we overcomplicate it. It's almost as if Jesus was saying to the crowd, "Guys, don't overthink this. You were lost. I love you. So I came looking for you. End of story."

Have you ever lost something valuable? If so, you know the pain and frustration that entails.

When we were getting ready to plant our church, I went on a twenty-one-day fast. It seemed like the spiritual thing to do, right? The problem is, I'm not very good at fasting. Is anyone, really? Maybe it's my fast metabolism or short attention span, but I have a tough time not eating between breakfast and lunch, much less for three straight weeks.

It was a liquid fast, and I stretched the definition of liquid as far as humanly possible. I'm not a legalist, so if the soup had some chunky stuff in it, I still ate it. I did juices. I did smoothies. I even did muscle milk. I don't think that's actually a liquid fast, but thank God for his grace. I tried hard.

One day I was sitting at a café working on my message for the coming Sunday service. I was so hungry I could barely think. I was convinced I was going to die. *This is horrible*, I thought. *Why did I do this to myself?* Suddenly an overwhelming feeling hit me. *I've got to eat. Right now. I've got to find some soup somewhere.*

I jumped up from the table. I left all my stuff there and headed out in search of soup. I wasn't even thinking coherently—I just knew I needed soup. I was like Esau in the Bible, trading my birthright for porridge. I finally found some soup at a nearby restaurant, and it warmed my soul. It was like manna from heaven. Liquid manna, but manna nonetheless. After I finished, I headed home.

The next morning when I woke up, I couldn't find my Bible or my computer. It was the strangest thing. I went through the whole house. I turned our home upside down. I was starting to flip out. I searched for hours.

Then I did what most husbands do when they can't find something on their own. I found my wife. "DawnCheré, where's my stuff? Where did you put it?" It's the process of elimination—if I can't find it, my wife must have moved it. Typical husband logic. I had a headache because I hadn't eaten, I was upset, I was blaming my wife. It was not my finest moment.

Suddenly the phone rang. I answered. It was the café where I had been the day before. "Mr. Wilkerson, did you happen to leave your Bible and computer here yesterday? We have them."

"Yes!" I just about lost my mind with joy. "But how did you know they were mine?" I asked.

"Well, your name is engraved on the Bible."

I felt slightly dumb. I definitely owed my wife an apology. "I'll be right there." I hung up, and I literally started dancing around the house. The Whip, the Nae Nae, and the Running Man had nothing on me. I went nuts in my own house, dancing because what had been lost was found.

Jesus' three stories illustrate the emotion of finding something that had been lost. It's a feeling we can all relate to, and Jesus' stories tell us what God feels when lost people are found.

The first story in verses 4–7 is about a shepherd who had one hundred sheep. One of them wandered off. Most of us would say at that point, "Well, you've got ninety-nine left. Cut your losses, count your blessings, maybe check the fence for holes, and move on."

Not this shepherd. He left the ninety-nine in search of the one. What? This was preposterous. This was crazy. This was illogical. Why risk ninety-nine to go after one?

Exactly. That was Jesus' point. Remember, he was giving his defense. He was explaining why he was the friend of sinners. And his point was, "I am obsessed with lost things."

The story gets even crazier. The shepherd brought the sheep back, and then he threw a party. What does that tell us? If the shepherd were a typical business-minded entrepreneur, he would have just tossed the sheep back in the pen, gone into his house, powered up his laptop, and updated his assets spreadsheet. No fanfare, no emotional outbursts, and certainly no extra expense for a party.

But this shepherd called all his friends. "Hey, party at my house. Come on over!"

"Why? What are we celebrating?"

"Remember that sheep I lost? I've been looking everywhere for him. I searched the countryside. I put up posters on telephone poles. I offered a reward. Guess what? I found him, and I'm out of my mind with joy. This deserves a celebration."

The sheep wasn't an asset, a number, or a statistic. The lost sheep was dear to the shepherd. There was an emotional connection. There was intrinsic value that went far beyond monetary worth.

More Than a Bagel: Parable of the Lost Coin

Jesus continued with his second story in verses 8–10. He told them about a woman who had ten coins. She lost one, and she turned her house upside down looking for it, similar to when DawnCheré misplaced my laptop. This woman didn't blame her spouse, though. (I know; I have issues.)

She found the coin and, just like the shepherd, she threw a block party. How much did she spend on that party? Maybe more than the value of the coin. Again, it was the illogical, over-the-top reaction that proved Jesus' point. Why did she search her house incessantly? Why did she throw a party? Because the coin had value to her.

There is a message in there for you and me. I don't know your background. I don't know what you've been through or what you've heard about God. I don't know what people have told you about yourself. But passages like this are a needed reminder that God values you infinitely and eternally. He values you more than others value you and more than you value yourself.

Where do you get your sense of value? From your accomplishments? From your education? From your family? From what others say to you or about you? A lot of us tend to derive our value from everything else other than God. Instead of getting our value from the *Word*, we try to get our value from the *world*. Ultimately that's a dead-end street. The world has no business defining your value.

As I said, I fly a lot. Even after all those trips, I still get nervous, especially in turbulence. The rumbling, the shaking, the sudden drops, the seatbelt light staying on for hours when I need to use the restroom—I hate it.

Once I was flying from New York to Miami. Everything was fine. There was a guy sitting next to me, but he hadn't asked me about my career, so we were cool. Then all of a sudden there was a massive *thud*. The lights went out, and smoke filled the plane. People began to panic. The guy next to me was yelling, "Oh my God, we are going to die!"

It bothered me that he was yelling like that because I was already panicking internally, and the added negativity didn't help. So I grabbed his arm and started yelling back at him, "Stop it! Just stop! We're not going to die. We're going to live!"

It was weird therapy, but it worked. "Okay," he whimpered. He grabbed my hand. Our fingers might have interlocked, and we shared a moment. The things you do in desperate times.

I've learned when you are in turbulence, you look at the flight attendants. They've been there before. So I always think,

If the flight attendants are cool, I'm cool. But what do you do when the flight attendants are panicking? Because they were clearly freaked out. My seatmate and I were still holding hands. We all thought we were going to die.

Then the smoke cleared a bit, and the pilot came over the loudspeaker. "Ladies and gentlemen, we are not sure what's going on, so we are making an emergency landing."

We landed in Raleigh, North Carolina. There were ambulances and fire trucks all over the place. It was evidently quite serious, but nobody explained anything to us. They booked us hotel rooms at the local Red Roof Inn. It offered a free continental breakfast. I was thinking, *Great. I almost died, and I get a bagel?*

We went to the hotel that night. The next day we got back on the plane—a different plane—and landed safely in Miami. After I landed, a friend sent me an article from the Raleigh newspaper. It said an airplane had been struck by lightning, one of the engines went out, and the plane was lucky to have landed safely. That was my plane.

Two days later I got an e-mail from the airline. It said, "Dear Mr. Wilkerson, because you are one of our trusted and preferred customers, we want to apologize to you for the slight delay a couple of days ago."

Slight delay? Do you mean my near death?

It continued, "Because of your delay, we have decided to credit your airline account ten thousand bonus miles."

Really? Ten thousand miles might get you a one-way ticket from Miami to Buffalo, New York, if you're lucky. Are you saying my life is worth no more than a bagel and a one-way ticket to Buffalo?

Obviously, an airline doesn't define my worth. But sometimes I am guilty of letting equally unqualified sources influence and inform my sense of significance. How often do I let people's off-the-cuff comments sabotage my self-esteem? How often do I let my performance define my self-worth?

Don't let the world dictate your value. You are not the sum total of what you have done or not done, of your talents and abilities, of your fame, of your behavior, of your morality. You are who God says you are, and he says you are fearfully and wonderfully made. He says all your days were ordained for you and written in his book before one of them came to be. He knit you together in your mother's womb. He knows every moment of your life, every dream, every fear, every success and failure.

This woman turned the house upside down looking for one coin. Why? Because it had value. Just because a coin is lost doesn't mean its value is lost. Every person on this earth—whether we have done good things, bad things, evil things, or beautiful things—is valuable to God; so valuable, in fact, that God sent his son on a death mission for us. We are worth *Jesus* to God. That is how much we mean to him.

> Every person on this earth—whether we have done good things, bad things, evil things, or beautiful things—is valuable to God.

Maybe you've felt overlooked and undervalued for a long time. Maybe you feel lost. Maybe you feel like you've missed your chance. Maybe you are rusty and dusty and abused. Please hear me: *God still says you are valuable.* Just as a coin gets its value from the government whose seal is stamped on it, so your value comes from the God whose image is emblazoned on your life. His concern for you, his valuation of you, and his passion for you never change.

Lost Boys: Parable of the Prodigal Son

Jesus' third story, in verses 11–31, is the most well-known of the three, and for good reason. It paints one of the most vivid and moving portraits of God the Father found anywhere in the Bible.

We often call this story the parable of the prodigal son, but Jesus didn't call it that. He started out by saying, "There was a man who had two sons . . ." (verse 11). We should probably call this the *parable of the two sons*, or the *parable of two lost boys*. Or maybe the *parable of the older brother who thought the story was about his younger brother but it was actually about him*. That's not quite as catchy, but it's probably closer to the point.

Remember who was listening to Jesus. Notorious sinners on one side, religious leaders on the other. Talk about a diverse audience. I can imagine Jesus looking at both groups and thinking, *I want you to know I am obsessed with both of you. Both of you are lost, but only one of you knows that. So I'm going to tell you a story about two sons. One is the prodigal, the runaway, the backslider; the other is the older brother. Both are equally far from God. Both are equally lost.*

You've probably heard the story. A father had two boys. The younger wanted his inheritance early. It didn't matter to him that the inheritance would probably be bigger if he waited until the proper time. It didn't matter to him that he was essentially saying, "Dad, I want your money more than I want you. I wish you were gone so I could have it all now." That's what sin does, by the way. It wants instant gratification. Eventually it turns us into selfish, shortsighted, and often mean versions of ourselves.

The father gave his son his inheritance. The boy promptly wasted it all with wild living. He threw some good parties. I'm sure he had a great time. But the problem with sin is it is only pleasurable for a season, and then the consequences catch up with you. Sin always promises more than it can deliver.

The boy became so poor he had to hire himself out to a pig farmer just to survive. But it wasn't enough. He was starving. One day he found himself longing for the scraps and swill he was feeding the pigs. At that point, the Bible says, he "came to his senses" (verse 17). Once again, Jesus was highlighting the absurdity of sin. Sin doesn't make sense. You get caught up in it, and then at some point you realize you are in a place you never planned to be. It robs you of the life God intended for you and leaves you abandoned, alone, desperate.

At this point the younger son had an idea. *I'll go home! Well, not home, exactly. I'll go back to my father and ask for a job. Obviously I can't be his son anymore. I messed up too much for that. But maybe he'll at least let me be a servant.* He starts to craft a speech in his mind. "Dad, I'm sorry . . ."

I can relate to the mental speech-writing thing. I used to sneak out sometimes in high school, and somehow my dad would always find out. I would come home, and I would always have a speech prepared. "See, Dad, what happened was, I fell out of the window . . ." Never really worked.

And neither did this speech, but for different reasons.

Something unbelievable happened when the son approached his house. Verse 20 says, "So he got up and went to his father. But while he was still a long way off, his father saw him and was filled with compassion for him; he ran to his son, threw his arms around him and kissed him."

That little phrase "a long way off" says so much about God's heart. God doesn't stand on the porch, cold and aloof, waiting for us to make our speeches and convince him we are sorry. Long before we were looking for him, he was already looking for us, waiting for us, full of love and compassion.

I am so thankful God looks for us when we are a long way away. Before I responded to an altar call, before I served at church, before I quit sneaking out of the house, before I decided to preach, before I went on a fast, before I pastored a church, God saw me in the distance.

Repentance is not an emotional thing. Repentance is not even a verbal thing. Repentance is making a simple turn toward God our Father. When you turn toward him, he *runs* toward you. Someone once said, "Slow are the feet of repentance, but swift are the feet of grace." You might be too embarrassed to look God in the face; you might be walking slowly toward him, crafting your repentance speech—but he is *running* toward you.

The son got to the dad, and before he could get his speech out, he found himself smothered in tears and kisses. That was the last thing he expected. He expected rebukes, maybe blows.

"Dad, wait. I have to tell you the bad stuff I did. I have to say sorry. I have to ask for a job . . ."

The dad completely ignored him. Then he said, "This calls for a party! Put a robe on my son. Put sandals on his feet. Put a ring on his finger. Hire a DJ. Invite the whole neighborhood.

Kill the fattened calf. We are going to throw the biggest party you've ever seen."

Have you ever wondered who has a fattened calf just hanging around? I think the Father does. For the moment when someone decides to turn to him. For the celebration he will have when someone decides to come home. Why? Because he is obsessed with finding what is lost.

Imagine Jesus sharing these stories with his listeners. One group of people had to have been thinking, *That's me, man. I ran away from God, and I ran hard. I did what I wanted. I listened to the lies of sin. I've done so many things—I don't even know how to start saying sorry. I've given up my right to be with God.*

Tears were probably coming down their faces. *I'm the prodigal son. No question about it. Jesus, are you saying God is running toward me? That he is full of love and compassion for me? That he will forgive me and give me a position in the family?*

Then Jesus turned to the other crowd. The religious crowd. And I think he felt the same love and longing he did toward the notorious sinners.

He started telling them about the older brother. The older brother had been out in the field working. He was clearly the responsible one. I'm sure the Pharisees perked up a bit. This was their guy. Surely Jesus was going to contrast the two and show how much better the older brother was than the younger.

The older brother could hear the dancing and music, so he called a servant to find out what was going on. "Your little brother is back, so your dad threw a party!"

The older brother was instantly angry. He couldn't believe his ears. This wasn't right. This wasn't fair. So he did what any mature person would do. He stayed outside and pouted.

His attitude toward the prodigal stands in clear contrast to the attitude of the father. And something tells me the Pharisees related a lot more to the self-righteous anger of the brother than they did to the running and the kissing and the celebrating of the father. After all, their biggest complaint about Jesus was that he accepted sinners.

If the younger brother is a picture of the deception of sin, the older brother is a picture of the deception of religion. You can know all about the Father, but that doesn't mean you have a relationship with him. You can live in the house but never have the heart of those who live in the house.

For the second time that day, the father went outside to find a lost son. The older brother complained, "Dad, I've always worked so hard for you. I've done everything you asked and more. If anyone deserves a party, it's me!"

To be honest, I've felt those emotions before. More times than I'd like to admit. It feels good to criticize bad people, to pat ourselves on the back, to throw a holy pity party and talk about how we deserve what we have and more. But those emotions, that attitude, completely miss the point.

Did the older brother deserve more than the younger brother? Yes . . . sort of. Sin has consequences, which is why the younger brother had suffered and lost so much. There were a lot of benefits to the older brother's lifestyle. Jesus' parable doesn't gloss over the effects of sin.

But ultimately, both brothers had their positions because they were sons. They didn't do anything to become sons—they were just born into the family. So talking about who deserved what was a bit petty compared to the fact that everything they had was a gift from their father.

That sounds a lot like grace. Where do we get the idea that our good works qualify us to pass judgment on people who have done a few less good works—or a few more bad ones? Why do we think we know who should get blessed and who should get judged?

The older brother completely missed the point. Sonship has nothing to do with deserving. If it did, it would no longer be sonship. It would simply be employment. Employees work for a *wage*. Sons work for the *family*. Employees work *for* position. Sons work *from* position.

If God's value system were based on works, then it would make sense to work, and to work hard. It would make sense to compare ourselves among ourselves, to rate and to rank, to jockey for title of Best in the Kingdom. But that's not God's value system at all.

The father replied to the older brother: "'My son,' the father said, 'you are always with me, and everything I have is yours. But we had to celebrate and be glad, for this brother of yours was dead and is alive again; he was lost and is found'" (verses 31–32).

Notice the little phrase "you were always with me." The New Living Translation says, "You have always stayed by me." What did the father value most about his older son? His hard work? His performance? His near perfection? I'm sure he valued those things too, but that's not what he chose to highlight. He looked his son in the eye and said, "Son, I'm so happy you're with me. And I'm so happy your brother is home now too. That's the most important thing."

What is God's value system? What motivates him? What makes his heart beat faster?

Relationship.

That is why he waited on the porch, eyes on the horizon,

hoping to glimpse the familiar form of his son returning. That is why he ran to him, embraced him, spoiled him. That is why he threw the party of the century. The verse says, "We *had* to celebrate." It wasn't an option or an afterthought. It was essential. Why? *Because his son was home.* And that's what matters to God.

Notice, the father had the exact same position and posture toward both children. He went out to meet the prodigal, and he went out to meet the older son. He invited them both into the house. He invited them both to the party.

Jesus has grace for those who have committed the crime, but he also has grace for those who judge the crime. Maybe you are the prodigal; maybe you are the Pharisee. Maybe your thing is legalism; maybe your thing is license. Maybe your sins have made you lost; maybe your self-righteousness has made you lost.

Maybe neither character in this story describes you because you have met the grace of Jesus and it overflows in you and through you to everyone you encounter. I hope so. That's my prayer and my desire in my own life. There have been times I've been a prodigal, and God has shown me what it means to be forgiven. There are times I've been a Pharisee, and God has gently reminded me I've missed the point, that he is the point, that his love is all that matters. I want to be obsessed with what Jesus is obsessed with: first, that he and I would be together; and second, that other lost people would be found.

> No matter who you are, what you've done, or where you find yourself, Jesus is ready to embrace you.

Lost sheep. Lost coin. Lost boys. Three lost things. Three outrageous parties. The point is clear. God is obsessed with finding what is lost because of his overpowering love for people. Remember what Jesus told Zacchaeus? "The Son of Man came to seek and save those who are lost" (Luke 19:10 NLT). That's his mission. That's his passion.

No matter who you are, what you've done, or where you find yourself, Jesus is ready to embrace you. And no matter who he brings into your path in the future, his grace is sufficient for them as well. Jesus is the friend of all.

CHAPTER 6

HE SEES YOU

IF YOU'VE EVER BEEN IN LOVE, YOU'LL know that love makes you do crazy things to be together. For example, I remember a love-inspired road trip I took during my freshman year of college. DawnCheré and I had been dating for less than a year. I was living in Cleveland, Tennessee. She was touring and singing at different events around the country.

One day she called, and we chatted for a while. She casually told me she was going to be in Washington, DC, a couple weeks later. She also happened to mention she would love to see me, but of course it was too far away for me to drive.

That was all I needed to hear. I decided I was going to be there no matter what. Washington, DC, was a long way from Cleveland, Tennessee, so I figured I needed a traveling companion. I decided to recruit my cousin, who was always up for an adventure. I called him up and told him my plan.

He replied, "Sounds fun! But Washington is a long way away."

"No, it's not that far. It'll be easy."

"How far is 'not that far'?" he asked suspiciously.

"A mere six hundred miles, bro. It's an easy nine-hour drive."

"You're insane."

I chose to take that as a compliment. "So you'll go?"

"Yeah, I got you, man. When do we leave?"

We left on a Thursday evening. Our plan was to drive all night. We would spend Friday and Saturday in DC. I would have two glorious days with DawnCheré, then we would leave Sunday morning.

Unfortunately, my car had other plans. It broke down. Twice. Our easy nine-hour drive turned into a thirty-six-hour ordeal that made us question our sanity and our Christianity.

We finally rolled into Washington sometime Saturday morning. We ended up spending barely a day there before we had to drive back. It didn't matter, though, because I was in love, and I got to see my girl. The time and effort were totally worth it. Worth it to me, at least—my cousin hasn't gone on a road trip with me since.

It's not just romantic love that makes us do crazy things for other people. Love makes a parent stay up all night with a newborn. Love gives a single mom the strength to work two jobs to support her family alone. Love motivates an elderly spouse to care for his wife for years in her old age. Love is not just a feeling—it is the force that draws us and binds us together.

Would I have braved sleep deprivation, mechanical breakdowns, and near-nervous breakdowns to drive from Cleveland, Tennessee, to Washington, DC, if I were not in love? Of course not. The trip would have seemed like a burden and an imposition. In retrospect, that's probably what my cousin felt. But from my perspective, it was easy. It was a no-brainer.

That's what love does: it longs to be close. It is compelled to draw near. Love will bridge any gap, travel whatever distance needed, to be with the object of love.

We shouldn't be surprised at the extreme lengths we go to, because God is love, and we were made in his image. He sent his son to die in our place so we could spend eternity together—that's as extreme as it gets.

Our God is not far off, hiding in heaven, aloof and unaware. No, our God is near. He came to us, he found us, and he restored us. Why? Because of his intense, overwhelming love.

In this journey called following Jesus, love is far more important than we might realize. Sometimes we think Christianity is about obedience. We think following Jesus is about gritting our teeth and trying to live holy lives, saying no to a lot of things we'd secretly like to do. But really, it's about love. The apostle Paul wrote this about the love of God:

> I pray that out of his glorious riches he may strengthen you with power through his Spirit in your inner being, so that Christ may dwell in your hearts through faith. And I pray that you, being rooted and established in love, may have power, together with all the Lord's holy people, to grasp how wide and long and high and deep is the love of Christ, and to know this love that surpasses knowledge—that you may be filled to the measure of all the fullness of God.
>
> (Ephesians 3:16–19)

In this passage, Paul told his readers what he prayed for when he thought about them: that they would understand and experience God's love. That's an interesting request, if you think about it. I don't usually pray that I would understand the love of God. I tend to pray for more tangible, urgent things like finances, health, or problems I'm facing. But Paul, one of the greatest figures in biblical history, prayed for something apparently simple yet ultimately profound: to know God's love.

Until we understand how much God loves us, we won't let God lead us. We won't let God help us. We won't draw near to him or let him draw near to us. Love is the force that brought God to earth, and it's the force that brings us to God.

The problem is we are often oblivious to the nearness of God. He is there, but we aren't aware of him. We don't recognize him. And, as a result, we find ourselves lonely, overwhelmed, and desperate.

Maybe we don't see God because we are distracted by the pressures and pleasures of life. We are oblivious to God not out of antagonism, but because our culture moves so quickly and shouts so loudly, we don't have the mental energy to think about God. We are just trying to catch up and keep up with the rush of life.

Other times we don't see God because pain and difficult circumstances are overwhelming our hearts and our senses. Maybe we believed he was close to us in the past, but life is suddenly contradictory, and we have trouble believing God could really be there.

This is why it is so crucial to understand and believe the love of God. Whether we are distracted or discouraged, whether we are panting at the pace of life or grieving over the losses of life, we need "to grasp how wide and long and high and deep is the love of Christ" (verse 18). It will be sanity for our souls.

Paul wrote about being "filled to the measure of all the fullness of God" (verse 19). Whatever we are full of is what we will be led by. The problem, by the way, is that a lot of us are full of other things. Some of us are full of anger, so we are led by anger. Some of us are full of bitterness, so we are led by bitterness. Some of us are full of ourselves, so we are led by selfishness.

The solution isn't to try harder to empty ourselves of these wrong things. It's to let God fill us with an awareness of his presence and his love. That's why Jesus came, to fill us with the right thing: the love of God. He came to reveal the love of the Father so that we could learn to love him back, to trust him, and to follow him. The nearness of God is motivated by the love of God, and his presence will carry us through every difficult season and every painful circumstance.

If being filled with God's love is so important, how do we perceive it and receive it? And how does it affect us? Here are three simple observations.

Sharing Our Feelings

I've met a lot of people—typically men, of course—who don't want to show emotion. They prefer to stay locked up, impassive, impervious, as if showing their feelings were a sign of weakness.

Not God. God has no problem expressing what he feels. He is an expressive, emotional, demonstrative God. He laughs. He gets jealous. He gets angry. His heart breaks. He feels compassion. He experiences grief.

Most of all, he *loves*. He expresses his love continually, not just with words, but with actions.

When I was a kid, we had a Christmas-morning tradition called the Santa Circle. My dad would dress up like Santa, and my three brothers and I would sit around the Christmas tree. One at a time, he would pass out presents to us. We would take turns opening them, everyone would clap, and the next brother would take his turn.

I remember one Christmas when I was about twelve years old. We were opening presents, but I wasn't getting what I wanted. So I developed a bit of an attitude, as only twelve-year-olds can. I would say "thank you" after each present, but my voice was dripping with sarcasm. There's nothing more annoying than a sarcastic preadolescent.

Keep in mind that when it came to respect and obedience, my parents didn't play. They would be like, "Rich, we will kill you, bury you in the backyard, and make another one, and no one will ever know you existed." They never said that, but when you're a kid, that's how you understand things.

My dad was trying to keep up the Santa façade, even though we all knew it was him. But finally he couldn't take it. He had this crooked finger that he would point at us when we were in trouble, and he pointed it at me. "Rich, change your attitude." Then he turned back to the family and said, "Ho, ho, ho!" And he was Santa again. It was a little hard to take him seriously in the suit and beard, I'm not gonna lie.

The circle came back around to me. I opened my present. Not what I wanted. So I said, even more sarcastically, "Gee. Wow. Thanks."

When I said that, it was on like Donkey Kong.

I remember attempting to convince him discipline was unjust. "Dad, I said thank you. Why am I in trouble?"

My dad replied, "Rich, you said thank you, but you didn't show gratitude."

What was he saying? That there is a big difference between *saying* something and *showing* it. Talk is easy. But talk is cheap. I love that God isn't just a talker; he's a doer.

John 3:16 is easily the most famous verse in the Bible. "For God so loved the world, that he gave his only Son, that whoever believes in him should not perish but have eternal life" (ESV). God didn't just tell us how much he loves us; he proved it with his actions, his sacrifice, and his generosity.

Giving is an action that expresses love. A relationship ends when giving dries up. Or, more accurately, when giving dries up, it means the relationship has ended. Why? Because you might be able to give without love, but you can't love without giving. Generosity is the inevitable result of love.

Some of us still don't understand the magnitude of God's gift. He sent us his very best. Notice the little word *so* in John 3:16. God *so* loved us. In other words, he felt such deep passion, such intense longing, that he was willing to do whatever was needed to express his love for us. He drew near to us when we couldn't draw near to him.

> You can't love without giving. Generosity is the inevitable result of love.

According to the Bible, we were all born with sinful natures (Romans 3:23). We have sin hardwired into us. Sin has one reward: death. That means the only thing you and I deserve is death. But God loved us so much, and he expressed that love by sending Jesus. Jesus didn't just die *for* you and me— it's better than that. He died *as* you and me on that cross. He became our sin so we could become his righteousness. He died so we could live and spend eternity with God.

I've heard 85 percent of communication is nonverbal, and my experience in a decade of marriage would tend to confirm that statistic. It's not what you say—it's how you say it. Husbands, take heed.

Most of communication is body language. It's posture. It's facial expressions. It's actions. When I ask my wife, "How was your day?" and she responds, "Fine," that doesn't necessarily mean it was fine. The tone of her voice is what tells me how it really went. Or when she does this certain gesture with her hair, it doesn't mean her hair is in her eyes. It means I'm in trouble. I learned that one the hard way. Or when she raises her eyebrows a particular way, she is saying, "I need to spend time with you. Now." There are a few nonverbal cues I love to see as a husband, but I can't put those in print. Married sex is the best sex, that's all I'm saying.

Jesus' death on the cross is God's greatest nonverbal communication. That's why the cross is more than a piece of jewelry or a fashion statement or a religious icon. It's a visual reminder of God's love for us. Jesus' crucifixion was an act of sacrifice, a way that God shouted without words, "See how much you are loved?! If you didn't get it with my words, look at my actions, at my posture, at my body language. I love you! I gave my one and only son for you."

You Experience Love

God has expressed his love by drawing near to us, but that's not enough to change our lives. Until we experience his presence, his awareness, his care for us on a personal level, we will remain unchanged.

I've met people who mentally agree with God's love, who verbally affirm it, who theologically prove it—yet who feel lost and alone. They know Jesus as master, teacher, and Savior, but they haven't met him as their friend. And when tough times come, their head knowledge is not enough.

I mentioned earlier how well-known John 3:16 is. The problem with familiarity, though, is that we can end up missing the personal significance of something. And, in this case, the danger can be compounded by the magnificent language of the phrase, "God so loved the world."

We can read that and think, *Wow, God is amazing! He loves the whole world. He's so big. His love is so great. Lucky world.* That's true. But I wonder, how often do we subconsciously dis-associate ourselves from the world? The term *world* is so macro, so big, that we can overlook ourselves. We are part of that world; therefore, God loved us so much that Jesus died for us. He's a big God. He's big enough to be small enough to be intimately acquainted with you and me.

When I was seventeen years old, my life was changed from the inside out. I answered the call of God. I've made a lot of mistakes since that moment, but I've never looked back. But it's only been in the last few years that I have begun to understand and believe that God truly loves *me*.

It's not hard for me to believe God loves you, but it is shock-ing that he loves me. Why? Because I know me. I know all about me. I've lived with myself for a long time, and I know the good, the bad, and the ugly. I could give you a list of reasons why I'm not worth that kind of love. Yet this verse tells me that God still loves me. How is that possible? This reality messes with me every time I consider it. It changes something. Actually, it changes *everything*.

There is an enormous difference between knowing about something and experiencing it for yourself. I'm sure you've heard about New York City, for example. You've probably seen movies filmed in New York. You've seen photos of the Manhattan skyline. Maybe you've read about it in a magazine, or studied its history, or heard facts about its population, culture, or traffic. You might even have an "I Love New York" sweatshirt. But if you haven't visited New York for yourself, you can't fully understand it. Not even close.

I could try to tell you about New York. I could write a book about New York. I could recount stories about New York. But at the end of the day, I can't explain to you what it feels like to walk through SoHo in the fall. I can't explain how it tastes to eat in the Italian district. I can't describe the scale and noise of Times Square. Anyone who has been to New York City will agree: you have to be willing to go there to truly experience it.

You might be wondering, *How do I experience God's love?* The same way: you have to be willing to go there.

You can go there in worship. You can go there in prayer. You can go there through the Bible. You can go there by thinking about God, listening to God, talking to other people about God. Open your heart to him. Live your life with him. Share with him the ups and downs, the worries and fears, the little details that define your day. God expressed his love; now you can experience it.

What I love about God's love is the closer you get to him, the more you learn about him. And the more you learn about him, the more you love him.

The same thing happens in human relationships, right? Love always means learning about the other person. That's what makes falling in love so exciting. I remember when I first met DawnCheré. We spent hours on the phone, learning about each other. "Oh my goodness. You like blue? Blue is my favorite color!" "You've eaten pizza? Wow, I love pizza!" The dumbest stuff ever.

That's the way relationships work. Learning leads to loving. Pursuing produces passion. It's not head knowledge, it's heart knowledge. We don't just learn facts about God—we experience his love for ourselves.

Sometimes, though, people think they know all they need to know about God. They've experienced him once, and that's enough. "Been there, done that." And when they start believing they know all there is to know about God, then their relationship with him stagnates.

Maybe you've experienced stagnation in a relationship in your life. You take someone for granted. You stop learning about him. You assume you know everything about her. A relationship like that—if you can even call it one—will eventually shrivel up. I've seen it happen in marriages, I've seen it happen in friendships, and I've seen it happen with people's love for God.

True love never stops learning because we can never know everything about another person. Relationship is the ongoing process of getting to know someone. That's what makes marriage so exciting: two people falling continually into love, learning and changing and experiencing each other over a lifetime.

It's what makes following

> Jesus' love is oceanic. It's bigger than you could imagine. His grace is deeper. His mercy is wider.

Jesus so exciting too. The closer I get to him, the more I realize how far away I was from him. The more I know him, the more I realize how little I knew him. Jesus' love is oceanic. It's bigger than you could imagine. His grace is deeper. His mercy is wider. You have to experience it for yourself—not through stories from your neighbor, or your mom, or your pastor. Yes, he loves the world. But you and I are the world.

We Evangelize It

Evangelism is one of those church terms that can be a bit weird to a lot of people. I grew up in church, and when I heard the term as a kid, it was often in a forceful, almost militant context: "Get out there and evangelize," or "You should be evangelizing more." Maybe that's the vibe you've gotten too, if you've spent much time in church. The unfortunate result is that for many Jesus followers, evangelism is both hard to understand and uncomfortable to do.

Even worse, the church has burned a few bridges with our culture in the name of evangelism. Church people are famous for forcing their beliefs and morals on people in the name of "witnessing." We have a reputation similar to telemarketers: pushing an unwanted message at inopportune times, and unable to take no for an answer.

I think we're overthinking it. Evangelism is so beautiful and natural that if you know Jesus, you're probably doing it without realizing it.

The term is based on a Greek word, and in the Bible it's usually translated "preach the gospel." That is still pretty religious-sounding, but *preach* just means tell or proclaim, and *gospel* means good news. So evangelism, at its heart, is nothing more than talking about the good news of Jesus' love.

God expressed his love, you and I experienced it, and now we get to share it with others. It's simple. It's also incredibly powerful.

What I especially love about this is that our message is *good* news. We live in a world full of bad news. Turn on the TV and flip through the news stations, and you'll get enough bad news in thirty minutes to last a month. Bad news in the Middle East. Bad news in the political system. Bad news in the economy. Bad news in your city. Maybe when you go to work, your workplace is full of bad news. Or when you go home, your home is full of bad news. Or you are in a relationship, and the relationship is bad news. Bad news seems to be this planet's default status.

Here's the thing, though. We might live in a world fixated on and frustrated by bad news, but we are not of this world. Once we know Jesus, once we have experienced the expression of his love, we are not full of bad news. We are full of good news: Jesus saves. Jesus sets free. Jesus is real, he is near, and he is ready to receive anyone who wants him.

He Knows Your Name

That brings me to John 20, which is an awesome chapter because it describes the first Easter. I love Easter. Not the pastel colors or sugar highs associated with it—I love what it symbolizes: Jesus' death, resurrection, and victory over death. Just to give you an idea of how much I love it, when we celebrated our first Easter as a new church, we dropped twenty thousand Easter eggs from a helicopter for local kids. Easter is, by definition, epic.

We celebrate Easter Sunday, which is the day Jesus rose from the dead. But there would have been no Sunday to celebrate without the most tragic Friday in history. Jesus died on Friday. From the luxury of our vantage point thousands of years later, we can call that day Good Friday because we know that Sunday was only two days later. But I guarantee you, none of Jesus' friends would have called it Good Friday when Jesus was crucified. They saw nothing to celebrate when his body was taken off the cross and laid in a grave. They didn't consider it good news when a stone was rolled in front of the tomb, the corpse of their best friend and their ultimate hope sealed inside.

Good news? Far from it. This was bad news. Sad news. Confusing news. Terrifying news. They thought Jesus was going to rule and reign in their lifetime. Many of them expected him to be a political ruler, the long-awaited deliverer who would free Israel from the control of the Roman Empire. Even more than that, Jesus was their best friend. He was their teacher, their role model, and their connection to the Father.

Jesus was *God*. How could God be dead? It didn't make sense. Their dreams were crushed, and their hearts were broken.

Early Sunday morning, two days after Jesus died and was buried, a woman named Mary Magdalene went to his tomb to pay her respects. To her shock, the stone that had sealed the tomb was gone, and the tomb was empty. She started to panic. Things were going from bad to worse. Jesus had been killed. Now even his body was gone?

Peter and John showed up next. They peered inside, then

stooped down and walked in for a closer look. Their fears were confirmed: Jesus' body was nowhere to be found. They left confused, wondering what this meant. A flood of conflicting emotions and thoughts must have overwhelmed their souls.

Mary Magdalene stayed at the tomb after the others had gone. I want you to imagine the scene because I think Mary represents many of us. The Bible tells us that earlier in her life, she had some serious issues. Jesus cast seven demons out of her, which would indicate she was pretty messed up. Her life had been radically transformed as she followed Jesus, though, to the point that she was one of the few people who stayed with him at the cross in his dying moments. Like all his disciples, she must have loved him and trusted him. She must have imagined a future with him as her God and her Messiah.

Now all that had come crashing down because Jesus was dead and gone. Mary must have felt anguished and abandoned. Good news? Not at all. God is near? He never felt farther. God's love and grace? Dead and buried along with her best friend.

Have you ever felt that way? I have. More times than I can remember. We know God is real. We know Jesus loves us. But then life throws us a curveball, and suddenly we feel alone. We feel abandoned by God. What happened to his promises? What happened to our dreams? Was it all an illusion, a false hope?

Mary couldn't hold back the pain. She began to weep in hopelessness and confusion. The apostle John described what happened next.

Mary was standing outside the tomb crying, and as she wept, she stooped and looked in. She saw two white-robed angels, one sitting at the head and the other at the foot of the place where the body of Jesus had been lying. "Dear woman, why are you crying?" the angels asked her.

"Because they have taken away my Lord," she replied, "and I don't know where they have put him."

She turned to leave and saw someone standing there. It was Jesus, but she didn't recognize him. "Dear woman, why are you crying?" Jesus asked her. "Who are you looking for?"

She thought he was the gardener. "Sir," she said, "if you have taken him away, tell me where you have put him, and I will go and get him."

"Mary!" Jesus said.

She turned to him and cried out, "Rabboni!" (which is Hebrew for "Teacher").

"Don't cling to me," Jesus said, "for I haven't yet ascended to the Father. But go find my brothers and tell them, 'I am ascending to my Father and your Father, to my God and your God.'"

Mary Magdalene found the disciples and told them, "I have seen the Lord!" Then she gave them his message.

(JOHN 20:11–18 NLT)

This story profoundly moves me, because I've been where Mary is. Not literally—I typically don't hang out in cemeteries and graves, empty or otherwise. But I've been in situations where the pain was so great, the brokenness was so real, I didn't know where to turn. I couldn't find Jesus in my hurt.

Have you ever tried to look through tears? Your vision is completely blurry. You can't see what's right in front of you because you are looking through a filter of pain and heartache.

Mary was desperate for Jesus, but her filter of bad news and grief was so real she didn't recognize him when she stared right at him. She even talked to him. "Gardener, sir, did you put Jesus somewhere?"

Sometimes our prayer life looks like that. "Jesus, where are you? I don't see you, Jesus. I don't feel you. Do you see me? Do you care about what I'm going through?" We can't see him, but we are talking to him. And he is close enough to touch.

There's a story about a fire that broke out in a family's home. The entire family escaped to the front yard except for one young boy, who was forced to flee to the roof. As flames crept up the side of the house, the boy's father stood below him and called up to him, "Son, jump! I'll catch you."

The boy approached the edge of the roof, but he could see nothing but flames and smoke. He drew back from the edge in fear. "I can't, Daddy. I'm afraid!"

His dad knew his son's life depended on him jumping, so he kept yelling, "Jump! I'll catch you. I promise."

"But, Daddy," the boy finally sobbed. "I can't see you."

The father replied, "But I can see you. And that's all that matters."

In this story, Mary was looking for Jesus. That was the right thing to do. But she couldn't find him. She couldn't see him. That's the condition so many people experience. They want God, but they can't see God, so they assume he is nowhere around.

Jesus had a flair for the dramatic, which is one more thing I love about him. He said just one word:

"Mary."

That was all it took. A familiar voice spoke her name, and something jumped in her heart. Suddenly she recognized him for who he was. "Teacher!" she cried out in joy. She raced to him, embraced him, to the point he had to tell her not to cling to him.

One word changed everything. One word dried her tears, repaired her dreams, healed her heart. One word changed bad news to good news to the best news. When she felt alone, Jesus was with her. When she felt like no one saw her need, Jesus was standing beside her, watching and caring. When she was grieving her loss, Jesus called her name.

Jesus knows your name. I said it before: God is both big and small. He's so big he can help you and so small he knows every detail about you. He is big enough to be small enough to be your friend and companion throughout life. In knowing your name, he knows everything there is to know about you. He loves you. He has a plan for you. He is watching over you.

Mary experienced his love and wanted to share it, so much so that Jesus essentially told Mary, "Don't hold on to me. Go and tell others about me." Again, it's the natural progression of God's love. He expresses it, we experience it, then we evangelize it.

The first witness of the gospel, the very first preacher of the gospel, was Mary Magdalene. She was a woman, which meant in that culture she had little public status or influence. She was an ex-demoniac, which means she probably had a past, a reputation, and a lot of baggage. But Jesus said, "Mary, you've seen me. You know my love. Your heart is full. Now let the love of God spill out to others."

That's how it works. We don't have to be weird to evangelize. We don't have to force ourselves to talk about Jesus for others to believe. We just need to let God's life and love overflow wherever we go. Sometimes that means talking, but often it just means loving and accepting people. It means enjoying life, because your joy and peace will make more people wonder what you've got—and how they can get it—than any sermon you could preach.

Mary went back to the disciples and said simply, "I have seen the Lord!" (verse 18 NLT). Then she told them what he said. From that moment on, things were different. The disciples eventually turned the world upside down with the simple revelation that Jesus was alive.

Jesus' teaching was incredible. His miracles were astonishing. But it was his resurrection that made all the difference. Don't underestimate the importance or power of that statement: "I have seen the Lord."

Maybe you are struggling with debt, and you can't find a way out. Maybe you are hiding an addiction and it's eating you up, but you don't know where to turn. Maybe your heart has been broken, and you wonder if you'll be able to go on. Maybe you wonder if God is real or if he cares about you.

Maybe you can't see Jesus through your tears, but he can see you. He's standing next to you, I promise. He is aware of what you are going through. He knows your pain, and he calls your name. Turn to him and see him for who he really is. Your life will never be the same because Jesus is near.

> **Maybe you can't see Jesus through your tears, but he can see you.**

CHAPTER 7

TEAR UP THE ROOF

I HAVE THE GIFT OF PROCRASTINATION. It's not a gift, I know—but wouldn't it be great if it were? What if putting things off until the last second were considered a positive character quality? I'd be a master in the fine art of instant gratification and delayed responsibility.

But it's not. It's a problem, which is why I intend to work on it. Tomorrow.

Actually, I've improved dramatically since my middle school years. By the time I hit high school and college, I was a relatively good student. But back in fifth grade—not so much. I remember sitting in class one day, and the teacher said, "Remember, tomorrow is the science fair." She had been announcing it for six months, but the day before was the first time it really clicked with me that I needed to have a project done.

I had nothing. No project, no planning, no ideas. So right then I decided to build a volcano. There is a famous volcano in Washington State called Mount St. Helens that erupted in 1980. I grew up in Washington, and everyone from that state knows the story of Mount St. Helens. This was part of my roots. It was perfect.

The only problem was, I had no idea how to build a volcano. Construction of any sort has never been my strong suit. I'm not a handyman and never will be. In my marriage, DawnCheré is the one with the tool belt. I'm helpless.

I had the overinflated confidence and independence of a middle-schooler, though, and I've always been strong-willed. There was no doubt in my mind I could pull off a six-month project in one evening. I talked to a friend, and he said, "Oh yeah, it's really easy. You make a base, you put paper maché around it, and then you use baking soda, vinegar, and food coloring to make it erupt. It's simple."

I went home and got to work. I had no idea how to make a base, and Google wasn't really a thing yet, so I just found an old orange parking cone. It was about three feet tall, so this was going to be a huge, very skinny volcano. I glued newspaper all around the cone and spray painted it brown. I don't think Mount St. Helens was brown when it blew up, but that's the color I had. Little orange blotches were creeping through the paper, but I didn't think it would matter. It was going to erupt and mess it all up anyway.

I found a cup and stuck it in the top. Then I looked through the pantry and located baking soda and vinegar. But we didn't have any food coloring. So I called my friend and said, "Do you have any red food coloring? This thing is going to look weird if it doesn't have lava. I don't want just fizz coming out."

He said, "Yeah, you want me to take it to school tomorrow?"

"That would be great. You won't forget?"

"No, man, I got you."

My dad was out of town, so the next day my grandpa drove me to school. I was still working on the volcano in the car. Once we got to school, I carried it into the gym. I had to keep re-assembling it because pieces were falling off. You could see large swaths of the orange cone underneath. It was a mess. Finally, my friend showed up. He had forgotten the food coloring.

Soon the judges came by my table and asked for a demonstration. I explained in about two sentences what Mount St. Helens was. Then it was time for the big moment. "Get ready for the volcano to erupt!" I said enthusiastically.

I mixed the ingredients, and white foam came out of the top. They were underwhelmed. "That's not lava."

"Yes, it is," I assured them.

Someone said, "I think your volcano is having a seizure."

I asked, "Can I finish it and bring it back tomorrow?"

"No. Sorry, it's too late." The judges marked my project incomplete. I watched all my friends get A after A, and I didn't even get a grade.

I learned a lesson that day about procrastination. I came face-to-face with the reality of deadlines, of due dates, of what happens when projects are overdue.

It's a valuable life lesson, of course. Projects have due dates, and part of growing up is discovering how to manage those due dates. So we learn to create to-do lists and calendars. We plot responsibilities out on time lines. We multitask; we project manage; we do what it takes to get stuff done.

That's a plus when it comes to the projects in our lives: schoolwork, jobs, home repairs, car repairs, debt repayment, starting a new business, buying a home, and so on. The problem is that sometimes the due-date mentality creeps into our attitude toward people. We place such a high value on "getting things done" that we subtly start to assume we can put people on our calendar. We want their hang-ups and weaknesses to conform to our time line paradigm, as if they were projects to be managed and delivered. And when our mental due date for them comes and goes, we are tempted to mark them incomplete and move on.

But people are not projects, and they don't have due dates. If a friend has a weakness, we can't calculate or control how long it will take him or her to change. We can't predict when a family member will finally break free from addiction. We can't set a deadline for someone's spiritual journey.

Projects can be managed, but people must be loved. Until we understand the difference between the two, we will have a tough time accepting other people, and we'll have a tough time understanding God's grace in our own lives. We will look at the lack of progress in someone's life and say, "Sorry, it's too late. Incomplete." And we'll give up on him or her. Since our (arbitrary) deadline has expired, we feel we no longer have any responsibility to accept or love that person.

> **Projects can be managed, but people must be loved.**

There is a story in the Bible that illustrates just how important it is to treat people as people, not projects. It's Mark 2:1–12:

When Jesus returned to Capernaum several days later, the news spread quickly that he was back home. Soon the house where he was staying was so packed with visitors that there was no more room, even outside the door. While he was preaching God's word to them, four men arrived carrying a paralyzed man on a mat. They couldn't bring him to Jesus because of the crowd, so they dug a hole through the roof above his head. Then they lowered the man on his mat, right down in front of Jesus. Seeing their faith, Jesus said to the paralyzed man, "My child, your sins are forgiven."

But some of the teachers of religious law who were sitting there thought to themselves, "What is he saying? This is blasphemy! Only God can forgive sins!"

Jesus knew immediately what they were thinking, so he asked them, "Why do you question this in your hearts? Is it easier to say to the paralyzed man 'Your sins are forgiven,' or 'Stand up, pick up your mat, and walk'? So I will prove to you that the Son of Man has the authority on earth to forgive sins." Then Jesus turned to the paralyzed man and said, "Stand up, pick up your mat, and go home!"

And the man jumped up, grabbed his mat, and walked out through the stunned onlookers. They were all amazed and praised God, exclaiming, "We've never seen anything like this before!" (NLT)

This story is about more than a spontaneous roof remodel. It is about how God views people and how we should view them as well.

We don't know much about the characters in this narrative. We don't know their names, their relationship to one another, or their opinion about Jesus. We don't know if they were good people or bad people. We just see a beautiful story of a few men who wouldn't give up on their paralyzed friend. And as a result, the friend had a radical encounter with Jesus, one that left him transformed inside and out.

It's important to remember in that day and culture, grave illness was often considered a sign of divine judgment. Popular belief said if a person was going through something this serious, it was because someone—either the person or the person's parents—had sinned. The sickness was punishment for some hidden fault.

What would that have meant for this paralytic? Many people would have shunned him, judged him, suspected him. "He must have done something terrible, and that's why he is like that. He must be a sinner. He deserves what he gets."

Not Jesus. The people society called sinners, Jesus called friends. The individuals labeled and discarded by culture were the people Jesus sought out. It was one of his defining characteristics, as we've seen throughout this book. So when the paralyzed man was unexpectedly dangling in front of him, I think Jesus was predisposed to help him. He had come to heal the sick, to restore the blind, to save the lost. This man was his mission.

The cultural mind-set I described above isn't as ancient and antiquated as we like to think. Two thousand years later, humans still tend to label and limit, to suspect and reject those who are struggling. I'm not talking about people struggling physically—although that happens too. I'm talking about internal struggles, moral struggles, addiction struggles, relational struggles.

I am so grateful that in a culture of rejection, Jesus is predisposed to help people in need. Why? Because I am a person in need. You are a person in need. Before we get any further in this story, we need to recognize that the paralyzed man represents each of us. Maybe we aren't in that condition now, but there was a time in each of our lives when we were lying on a mat, helpless, hopeless, and desperate.

One reason Jesus followers can lack compassion for struggling people is because they don't remember, or never experienced, what life was like without Jesus. They've forgotten how much God has done in their lives. They believe their positive changes and good morals are the result of their own hard work and remarkable self-discipline.

This man was paralyzed. I can't think of a better visual for life before Jesus. Please don't misunderstand me: this metaphor is not meant to reflect negatively on people who deal with paralysis. I know people who have overcome incredible odds and challenges in the physical realm, and they live full and happy lives. But as a spiritual illustration, paralysis is a very descriptive picture of life without Jesus.

To be paralyzed means parts of your body don't work properly. If your legs are paralyzed, it affects your walk. If your arm or hand is paralyzed, it affects your actions. If your face is paralyzed, it affects your speech and your expressions.

In the spiritual realm, that's what life is like without Jesus. You can't walk into abundant life. You can't act the way you want or accomplish the things God has placed in your heart. Words and emotions easily become unhealthy and harmful. So when people in our lives who don't know Jesus say or do wrong things, our first reaction shouldn't be to avoid them, preach at them, or shame them. They are probably doing the best they can, but life without Jesus is like living with paralysis.

Can you imagine walking up to someone who is paralyzed and saying, "Come on, get up and walk! What's wrong with you? You just need to try harder." That would be ridiculously offensive. Yet we do essentially the same thing when we tell people to pull themselves together morally, to just try harder to be better. Isn't it a little arrogant on our part to assume they haven't already tried that?

Have you ever attempted to communicate with someone who doesn't speak your language? What do you do when the other person doesn't understand you? I've heard many English speakers respond a particular way in this scenario: they talk louder. They practically shout. "*How! Are! You! Doing!?*" It makes me laugh so hard. It's totally illogical. Volume is not the problem, and yelling is not the answer.

Often that is what the church looks like. "Come on, get up! What's wrong with you?" we metaphorically shout. Then we wonder why the person doesn't respond. The real response should be one of compassion. It should be a broken heart. "I am so sorry for what you are going through. I'm here to carry you. I'm here to help you. I'm here to take you to the one who has the answer—his name is Jesus."

If you've been following Jesus for a while, I think it's healthy to take a moment to imagine what your life would look like without him. My guess is that it would be a lot like the lives of everyone around you who don't know Jesus: family members, coworkers, neighbors. Were it not for Jesus, we would have the same limits and struggles, or worse. Until we get God's perspective of hurting people, we won't help them. We'll just judge them and shun them. We might even block the doorway so they can't get through.

Yes, people have problems. Why does that shock and appall us? So did we. So *do* we. That's what sin does. It steals, kills, and destroys. It robs our humanity and twists our identity. It paralyzes us. We know that already—so let's stop freaking out about people's issues and instead help them meet Jesus. Let's be friends of sinners.

Everyone Is Welcome

The house in this story was full beyond capacity. It would have made a fire marshal cringe. You couldn't fit one more person in (at least not using traditional means—we'll get to the dramatic roof entrance in a moment). Word had gotten out that Jesus was at this particular home, and people in need packed the place out.

I love the image of a full house because it reveals Jesus' passion for the world. His heart is broken for a broken humanity. All are welcome; he won't turn anyone away. Two thousand years later, the same thing happens. People all over the world gather to find answers in Jesus. They gather in homes; they gather in churches; they gather at coffee shops. Jesus is still a sellout because he is still the answer.

As our church has grown, I hear comments once in a while that make me uncomfortable. "This church is getting too big. There are so many people. I don't know everyone. Is my purse even safe? The parking lot is too full. I have to get here early to find a seat."

Stories like the one about the paralyzed man remind us there is no such thing as a church that is too big because people are more important than comfort. Jesus didn't die on the cross for "us four and no more." By big or small, I'm not talking about an attendance number either—I'm talking about a mentality that says, "I'm good, I'm comfortable here, so we need to close the doors before anyone else comes in."

I went to a Justin Bieber concert a while back in Tulsa, Oklahoma, and I had this thought as I looked around at the sold-out, packed arena: *I hope one day our church looks like this.* I could visualize the arena filled with people coming to meet

Jesus. I could imagine all that noise and craziness coming from individuals gathered to worship God.

You might ask, "Why, Rich? Do you just want big crowds? Big numbers? Fame?"

Of course not. The idea of a church that big is scary, actually. I dream about packed houses for one reason, and one reason only: because there are so many people who want to see Jesus, and I want to provide space and opportunity for that encounter.

Think how sad it would have been if this man went home still paralyzed because he couldn't get to Jesus. I love Justin Bieber, but Justin can't save your soul. He can't deliver you. If you get sick and go to the hospital, the Biebs isn't going to visit you. The only one who can be there in every moment is Jesus. He is the answer, so let's pack our churches talking about him.

The point, of course, is to reach both the many and the one. We've probably all felt what it's like to be lonely in a large crowd. The goal isn't numbers; it's people. The goal isn't having big churches; it's being big people. It's becoming big-hearted, arms-wide-open followers of Jesus who always have room for one more. People aren't projects. They are just—people. Men, women, young, old, sinners, saints, well-behaved, not-so-well-behaved. They should be welcome in our churches, in our homes, in our social circles, and in our hearts. Every single one is welcome with God, so every single one should be welcome with us.

Maybe you have no trouble accepting people with problems because you have more problems than anyone. Your tendency isn't to avoid sinners, it's to avoid church or to avoid Christians. Maybe you've tried Christianity before, and you were labeled, judged, and discarded. If that's the case—I'm so sorry.

Let me say this loud and clear: you are welcome in God's family. It doesn't matter if you have issues, hang-ups, addictions, or doubts. Your past might haunt you, your present might embarrass you, or your future might scare you. Jesus still welcomes you. There is always room for one more.

Let me say this loud and clear: you are welcome in God's family.

Treadmill Christians

I mentioned earlier that the paralyzed man represents each of us before we came to Jesus. We are not just the paralyzed man in this story, though. I believe God wants us to be like the four friends. He wants us not only to receive our own healing, but also to help others find wholeness in Jesus.

These men demonstrated two exceptional qualities that describe what our attitude should be toward people around us. First, they were *committed*. They scaled a house, demolished a chunk of roof, and dropped someone through the hole commando-style. That's intense. That's laborious. They weren't bored one day, looking for something to do, and accidentally found themselves on a roof. No, this was intentional. They had made a decision to do whatever it took to get their paralyzed friend to Jesus.

It would have been understandable if these men had simply wished their friend the best and continued with their lives. After all, his condition appeared to be permanent. And as we saw before, a lot of people assumed it was his own fault anyway.

But there was something in these men that made them not only notice their friend's need, but do something about it.

Are we aware of the needs of those around us? Do we care enough to be committed to their well-being? Commitment comes from concern, and concern arises from awareness. The first step in becoming a friend like these four men is to open our eyes to those around us.

I'm not talking about being a busybody, sticking our noses in other people's business. I'm simply talking about being alert to the people who are looking for help, desperate for answers, willing to open their hearts to us. I'm especially talking about people with whom we have a relationship, maybe not a close relationship yet, but one that could develop if we allow ourselves to really listen to them, to feel their pain, to hear their hurt.

The four friends were so committed, they carried their friend to Jesus. That turned out to be a little more complicated than they originally thought.

"Guys," one of them must have said. "Jesus is back in town! He's done all kinds of miracles. Crazy stuff. Maybe Jesus could heal him!"

"Great idea! How do we get him there?"

"I was thinking we'd carry him. It's only a couple miles away."

"Right! Let's do it. How hard could it be?"

A couple hours later they found themselves perched on top of a house, balancing a guy between them while they built a sky-light. It wasn't what they had planned, but they saw the process through. Why? Because they were committed to a person, not a project. It didn't matter how long it took or what it cost them personally, they were going to carry their friend to Jesus.

A few years ago I was at Disney World with one of my

nieces, who was about two years old at the time, and she suddenly decided she was incapable of forward motion. Funny how that happens with small kids. "I can't walk," she groaned.

"You're fine," I said. I wasn't really interested in standing still for the rest of the day.

"No, I can't walk. My legs are broken."

"Fine, I'll carry you," I said. I put her up on my shoulders. Five minutes later, I thought I was carrying my cross. I couldn't believe how heavy she was.

Carrying people is often challenging. It's easy to say we love people, and it's easy to pray for people, but are we willing to go to where they are, stoop down, and help them get to Jesus? Carrying people can be slow. It can be tiring. It can be inconvenient. But look at the result: a man with no hope and no ability to save himself found freedom greater than he could have imagined.

If we aren't careful, we can be what I call treadmill Christians. You might enjoy treadmills, you might not. Public opinion is split on them, I've discovered. Personally, I have a love/hate relationship with treadmills: I used to love them, but now I hate them.

I'm not sure at what point things changed. When I was going to college in Cleveland, Tennessee, I loved exercising on a treadmill. I'm not trying to brag here, but I had built up a reputation. I was the treadmill king. I don't think anyone actually called me that, but that was how I saw myself. I would go into the gym, and I'd have my whole Nike outfit on: Dri-FIT ankle socks, Roshe shoes, running shorts, training top, and of course my iPod and water bottle—I was ready.

I'd start out slow. The air-conditioning would be on. I'd watch ESPN while I walked. Eventually I'd start running, and I would dominate that treadmill. People would walk by, and I'd look down from my lofty moving belt. "Hey. Hi. Good to see you. Yeah, I'm the treadmill guy. The treadmill king."

One day a star player on the girls' soccer team was in the gym. She was dating one of my best friends at the time. She came over to me and said, "Rich, we've heard about you. We've heard about your treadmill ways."

I said, "I'm not surprised. Many people have."

"Would you like to go on a run with the girls tomorrow?" she asked.

"Yes, I'd love to," I said. "What time do you want to meet at the treadmills?"

"Um, no, Rich. We're not going to run on treadmills."

I was confused. "Where do you plan on running?"

She replied, "We'll run outside."

"Outside? Never heard of outside."

She said, "Meet us at the soccer field at 4:00 p.m."

"All right, let's do this. See you there. Outside."

The following day I discovered there is a big difference between running on a treadmill and running outside. Outside, the elements assault you: rain, sun, wind, tornadoes. Cars attempt to run you over. Dogs bark at you and almost bite you. Rocks intentionally trip you. Girl soccer players run by and mock you. It's rough.

I got destroyed that day, and it wasn't even a race. They were just out for a jog, but I couldn't keep up. Have you ever exercised so hard you convinced yourself you have tuberculosis? That was me, running outside.

Here's my point. We can be Christian treadmill kings. We think we are awesome, we are working hard, we are successful, we are spiritual—but we aren't actually using our faith in the real world, with real people and real problems. We are just walking in place, enjoying the accolades and the air-conditioning.

Jesus didn't die on a cross so we could be treadmill Christians. He wants us to get out there and get something done. Many of us know more Hillsong tunes than we know what to do with. We have half our Bibles highlighted. But if we don't live what we know in the real world, what's the point? We can talk the talk, but can we walk the walk? Can we be committed to people? It's time to get off the treadmill, go find someone in need, and commit to them. "How can I serve you? How can I help you? How can I be a better friend?"

This paralyzed man was alone and helpless. Then suddenly four guys came around him. They picked him up. They carried him to Jesus. He went from having two bad legs to having eight good legs, and his life was never the same. Let's be people committed to carrying one another.

People Are Worth It

These four friends weren't just committed; they were also creative. Commitment can turn into hardheadedness if it's not paired with creativity. The goal isn't to force solutions but to find solutions. Entering through the roof definitely qualifies as "thinking outside the box." It was innovative and effective, so much so that we are still talking about it today.

This is one of those Bible stories we often read quickly without really imagining the scene, but it's worth taking a moment to think about. It was so crazy, so over the top, that I'm sure the disciples laughed about it for years to come. The story made it into several of the gospels, so clearly it left an impact. Some scholars say it's probable this was Peter's house, which makes the story even better. I'm sure he had a few choice words to say that day.

Imagine if you were one of the disciples in this scene. People were packed in everywhere. There was no room to move. Jesus was healing the sick, answering questions, and teaching about God; it was unlike anything the people had ever seen. The atmosphere was electric.

Then, over the noise of the crowd, an odd sound began to emanate from the roof. At first it was just scratching. "Peter, you've got rats again," I can imagine John saying. Then the scratching turned into banging. Dust started falling in people's eyes and beards. And along with the noise coming from the roof, there were voices. So much for the rat theory.

Soon, more than dust started falling down: chunks of clay and pieces of tile were raining into the middle of the now completely distracted crowd. Peter had to have been freaking out. There was a mess everywhere. How was he going to explain this to his wife?

After a few more bangs and scrapes, an actual hole appeared in the roof. Daylight streamed in, illuminating the dust in the air. Against the sky, the silhouettes of four figures could be seen, energetically moving tiles and widening the hole. They seemed to be talking to someone. "Hang on, buddy. Almost there. This is going to work. This is going to be great."

I can imagine Peter's protests. "What are you *doing*? You can't just dig a hole in my roof! I'll take your ear off, dog, you know I will!"

Nothing deterred these men. Not the mess, not the mockery, not the grouchy homeowner. In order to help someone no one else was helping, they had to do something no one else was doing.

Here's the lesson in all this: *people are worth it*.

"Worth what?" you ask. Worth everything. Worth the mess and the chaos. Worth the effort and the expense. If we are committed to helping people, we have to engage our creativity. If we want to reach people no one else is reaching, we have to do things no one else is doing.

I want to be the kind of person who digs holes in roofs. I want to be part of a community, a church, that digs holes in roofs. Why did our church do a reality show a couple years ago? We were digging a hole in a roof. Why did we drop twenty thousand Easter eggs from a helicopter? We were digging a hole in a roof. Why do we have the stage, the lights, the music, the vibe we have? We are digging a hole in a roof. We are helping people see Jesus who might not see him any other way.

I find that often a lack of creativity is really just a lack of effort. Sometimes we hear a message about helping people, about telling them about Jesus, and we immediately start going through a list of reasons why we can't do that right now. "It's not my spiritual gift." "I'm in a different stage in life." "I'm called to pray." Some people are more creative with their excuses than with their efforts to reach people.

You don't need to pray about whether you should help hurting people. Just read the Bible. Love is your calling, and love gives, love helps, love serves. If you have to pray about whether or not you should love on people with the love of Jesus, you've missed something. Don't overthink it or over-spiritualize it. Quit praying; start obeying.

The reality is that when you follow

> Love is your calling, and love gives, love helps, love serves.

Jesus, you'll start to notice paralyzed people. Often you won't even be looking. It might even be someone you've seen a thousand times, but suddenly you'll see past the façade and realize his anger, her cynicism, are simply the side effects of not knowing Jesus.

Something in your heart will jump, and you'll find yourself feeling compassion. Instead of reacting to their negativity or recoiling at their sin, you'll see yourself in them. God's love will flow through you, and you'll find yourself doing things, saying things, and befriending people you never would have imagined.

Compassion will lead you to commitment. And commitment will produce creativity. You'll go from critical outsider to close friend. You'll find yourself doing whatever it takes to reach people, help people, heal people.

Group Faith

The Bible tells us something profound about what motivated Jesus to intervene in this man's life. Verse 5 of Mark 2 says, "Seeing their faith, Jesus said to the paralyzed man, 'My child, your sins are forgiven'" (NLT).

Notice whose faith caught Jesus' attention: "*their* faith." Jesus didn't just see the man's faith; he saw the friends' faith as well. There were four other dudes who had hope, faith, and expectation that Jesus was going to do something for their sick friend. In other words, miracles are often a group project.

Maybe you can relate because you know you should be dead, but there was a grandmother who never left her knees. She prayed for you when you couldn't care less about prayer. Maybe you should be in jail, but your mom kept praying and believing you would find Jesus. Their faith mattered.

Something powerful happens when we have faith for other people. God takes notice, and he does impossible things on their behalf. *Your* faith matters. If you are that mom praying for your boy, don't stop. If you are that grandmother, keep believing for the prodigal grandson or granddaughter. If you are a teenager praying for your parents' marriage, don't give up. If you are a college student still hoping against hope your dad can break free from the sexual addiction that is ruining his life, keep praying.

Don't put people on time lines; don't stamp expiration dates on them; don't grade them "incomplete" and move on. Have faith that God can intervene even when your patience long ago ran thin.

Often we think we have to change people; we assume the burden is on us to fix them. Our motivations might be good, but our goal is way off. We can't change anyone. We can't even change *ourselves* most of the time. Only God can heal a paralyzed person; only God can forgive sins.

Our problem is we want God to love them, and we want to change them. How about if we just love them and let God change them?

The First Miracle

Notice how Jesus fixed the eternal before he fixed the temporary in this story. When he said, "My child . . . ," everyone must have leaned in, expecting a dramatic miracle. The young man himself must have thought, *This is it! I think he's going to heal me. This is going to be awesome.*

Then Jesus continued, "Your sins are forgiven."

I think the young man was confused. *Um, thanks? I'm not sure what you're talking about. I just want to be healed. I just want to walk.*

What was Jesus doing? He was meeting a greater need than anyone else could have foreseen. The young man, his friends, and presumably the entire crowd were hoping Jesus would heal his paralysis. He clearly needed it. This was Jesus' big moment, his chance to prove his divine power. And he chose to forgive sins? Was he trying to let people down? No—he was making a point.

The greatest miracle in this story isn't the physical healing. Not even close. It's the spiritual one. Jesus knew the real problem this young man faced was sin. It was separation from God. So he spoke one phrase, and heaven welcomed a sinner into the family. The first and best miracle here was one no one could see.

The Pharisees reacted like Pharisees do: with self-righteous indignation and theological arguments that missed the obvious. They said, "Only God can forgive sins" (verse 7 NLT).

Exactly, Jesus must have thought. *I couldn't have said it better myself.*

Jesus didn't say it in so many words, but it was clear to the crowds. God was in the house. And his power was present not just to fix temporary problems, but to fix eternal ones.

The Pharisees' theology couldn't handle the declaration, "Your sins are forgiven." They were certain the man couldn't walk because of his sin. So how could he be forgiven and yet still not walk? How could he be flat on his back if he were truly free from sin?

Often we think the same thing. We want measurable, visible changes in people's lives. And until we see those changes, we have a tough time believing certain people are good with God. We need to remember what the Pharisees forgot: although people might still be on their backs even after meeting Jesus, they are already forgiven. They are on a journey with God, and he is doing something on the inside.

Dad Helped Me

After calling out the Pharisees, Jesus healed the man's body. It was dramatic, epic, memorable. And it made his point even clearer. He is God; therefore, he can forgive sins and heal bodies. He does the hard part, the impossible part. All we can really do is bring people to Jesus. It is Jesus who forgives, heals, gives purpose, saves, and restores.

When I did my volcano science fair project back in fifth grade, I remember watching my classmates walk in with their projects. My volcano was a disgrace to volcanoes and science fairs everywhere, but some of my friends had projects that looked way too good to be the product of a fifth grader. One kid had a solar system with black lights, fans, and theme music. Another guy had a volcano that actually erupted.

I asked them, "How did you pull those off? They look amazing."

They all had the same reply: "My parents helped me."

I remember thinking, *I should have asked my dad for help a long time ago. This was too much to do on my own.*

I also should have started my project earlier than twelve

hours before it was due, but that's not my point. My point is that when it comes to people, we need to ask God for help. It's too much to do on our own. No matter how much planning, preparation, or work we put into people, we can't control the outcome. God has to do the work in their hearts.

We are called to help take people to Jesus. He is the only one who can bring life and hope to a world in need.

PART 3

CHURCH: THE MISSION
OF THE BELIEVER

IN THE FIRST SECTION OF THIS BOOK, WE looked at the scandalous message of Jesus: his grace, his acceptance, and his love for everyone. Our good intentions and good efforts could never be enough, but he is enough. He is more than we deserve, and he is all we need.

Then, in the second section, we talked about God's passion for the world and culture we live in. God is an active God. He is obsessed by a love for humanity. That's why he sent Jesus: to save the world and to restore the world to friendship with him.

Now I want to take several chapters to look at our calling as followers of Jesus, as the church Jesus established. If Jesus is the friend of sinners, and if he loves the world so much that he gave his life to save us from sin, what does that mean for us? What is our response? What is our calling?

Simply put: the role of the church and of each of us is to be the friend of sinners. It's not to "get people saved"—only God can save. It's to allow Jesus' love to flow through us to other people. In the next few pages, you'll learn some practical keys to being the kind of friend Jesus was. It's a lot easier than you might think, and it's incredibly fulfilling. There is nothing in all the world like seeing someone find freedom and forgiveness in Jesus.

CHAPTER 8

WELCOME TO THE
NEIGHBORHOOD

I LIVED IN TACOMA, WASHINGTON, UNTIL
I was fourteen years old. Even after all these years, I have vivid memories of several of our neighbors.

There was one kid in particular, a bully who beat me up regularly. I'll call him Aaron. I'm changing his name to protect the guilty. I did my best to keep peace, to avoid conflict, but it didn't seem to help. He found me and pummeled me all the time.

I used to go home after my encounters with Aaron the bully and tell my dad about him. He would say, "Rich, you've got to love Aaron with the love of the Lord."

I remember thinking, *The love of the Lord? What does that even mean?*

Another neighbor, an older gentleman we'll call Tom, also stands out in my nightmares—er, memory. He was the stereotypical grumpy neighbor, and apparently I was his Dennis the Menace. I am convinced he stood vigil at his window, silently daring neighborhood kids to tread upon a corner of his yard. The instant we did, a gravelly voice would holler from somewhere unseen, "Get off my grass!" My cousins and I would conduct experiments, stepping into his yard at different times of the day, just to see if he was watching. He always was.

Every single Fourth of July during my entire childhood, Tom called the police to report we were lighting off fireworks. We were, of course, but so was everyone. We were celebrating independence, freedom, and American pride, and the logical way to do that was to blow stuff up. He never got it. He called the cops every time.

When I complained to my dad about Tom, Dad would say, "Rich, love him with the love of the Lord." So I would try my hardest to love him, only to give up and settle for resenting him silently.

There was an old song we used to sing in church that used that phrase, "I love you with the love of the Lord." You'd usually smile at the person next to you while singing, as if you were telling them how much you loved them. Not romantic love, of course—it was strictly the love of the Lord. But it was a little creepy, to be honest.

I assumed that was what Christians said when we were trying to tolerate someone we didn't like. Only God could love a person like that, so we said, "I love him with the love of the Lord." I thought it was Christian code for "I can't stand that person, and I wish the Lord would take him now."

My grandparents were also our neighbors. They lived right next door to us, and unlike Aaron and Tom, they were amazing. My grandmother taught me piano, she cooked for us, my grandfather drove us to school every day—they were the best. When

I knew I was going to be in trouble for something, I'd run over to their house. "Nana, Mom's going to beat me up!" Grandma would fight my battles for me. It was awesome. I loved going to their house. Best neighbors ever.

My memories of our Tacoma neighbors have always colored my understanding of a famous parable Jesus told. It's usually called the parable of the good Samaritan, but it could have also been titled "Who's My Neighbor?" Here's how the Bible records the parable and its context in Luke 10:25–37:

> And behold, a lawyer stood up to put him to the test, saying, "Teacher, what shall I do to inherit eternal life?" He said to him, "What is written in the Law? How do you read it?" And he answered, "You shall love the Lord your God with all your heart and with all your soul and with all your strength and with all your mind, and your neighbor as yourself." And he said to him, "You have answered correctly; do this, and you will live."
>
> But he, desiring to justify himself, said to Jesus, "And who is my neighbor?" Jesus replied, "A man was going down from Jerusalem to Jericho, and he fell among robbers, who stripped him and beat him and departed, leaving him half dead. Now by chance a priest was going down that road, and when he saw him he passed by on the other side. So likewise a Levite, when he came to the place and saw him, passed by on the other side. But a Samaritan, as he journeyed, came to where he was, and when he saw him, he had compassion. He went to him and bound up his wounds, pouring on oil and wine. Then he set him on his own animal and brought him to an inn and took care of him. And the next day he

took out two denarii and gave them to the innkeeper, saying, 'Take care of him, and whatever more you spend, I will repay you when I come back.' Which of these three, do you think, proved to be a neighbor to the man who fell among the robbers?" He said, "The one who showed him mercy." And Jesus said to him, "You go, and do likewise." (ESV)

Jesus told the lawyer that the entire law—in other words, everything needed to live holy and please God—was summed up in two commands: love God and love your neighbor (verse 27). When I see that, I immediately think of my grandparents. What's not to love there? They were the best. Of course I love *those* neighbors.

The rest of my neighbors—not so much. Which of course sparks the question, "Jesus, who are you talking about, exactly? Which neighbors? Because there are neighbors, and there are *neighbors*, if you know what I mean, Jesus."

The lawyer had that exact question, and the parable of the good Samaritan was Jesus' reply. There's a good chance you've heard this story if you've been in church for any length of time. I'd like to invite you to reexamine it with me, though, in light of our overall theme: that Jesus is the friend of sinners.

Here's why. If we try to love the "interesting" people in our lives the way I tried to love Aaron and Tom, we'll probably be as frustrated as I was as a kid. How do you love people when they beat you up and call the cops on you all the time? Is it just a matter of singing, "I love you with the love of the Lord" and continuing to resent them in your heart?

I think there is more to it than that. The answer to loving our neighbors is found in understanding God's heart toward humanity. We have to see what motivated him to take the initiative to be a friend of sinners.

Neighbors at War

To understand the full impact of this story on hearers, we need to know the historical context. More than nine hundred years before the time of this story, Israel went through a civil war and split into two countries. The northern part kept the name Israel, while the southern part took the name Judah.

Two hundred years after that, a foreign nation by the name of Assyria conquered the northern kingdom of Israel. They deported many inhabitants of the land and repopulated it with people from other conquered nations. Over the following centuries, the original Israelites intermarried with the newer inhabitants. They adopted many aspects of the cultures and religions of the other ethnic groups. As a result, they were no longer "pure" Jews, either in bloodline, beliefs, or behavior. This region became known as Samaria, and the inhabitants were Samaritans.

The southern nation of Judah lasted a couple hundred years longer, but eventually they, too, were conquered, this time by the nation of Babylon. Judah preserved its purity better than the north, though, and eventually reestablished themselves as a nation. They followed the ancient beliefs handed down to them from Abraham, Moses, David, and other Hebrew heroes. They kept the law, worshipped at the temple, and did their best to obey the one true God.

Fast-forward to the time of Jesus. Now Rome was the ruling world power, and both Judah and Samaria were their subjects.

They were neighboring nations, but there was a centuries-old rift between them. First the original civil war, then centuries of conflict, plus massive cultural and doctrinal differences—it was a mess.

The "true" Jews from Judah detested and despised their northern Samaritan neighbors with holy zeal. They felt divinely justified in their hatred because Samaria represented sin, impurity, and mixture, which was the antithesis of a holy God. It was racism and prejudice in its most blatant form. The Jews avoided Samaritans, made fun of Samaritans, and discriminated against Samaritans. They treated them as second-class citizens and as enemies.

Jesus was intentional about the characters he chose for his story. First a priest, a trusted and respected figure in the community, ignored the man in need. Then a Levite, who also would have been respected, did the same. The audience at this point must have been wondering, *If the priest and Levite didn't stop to help, who will? This guy has no hope.*

Then came the real plot twist: a Samaritan. I'm sure there was an audible gasp from the audience. *A Samaritan?* They must have wondered, *Why is he in the story?*

At the very least, they would have expected the Samaritan to be as indifferent as the priest and Levite. Some of them probably thought he was going to be the villain of the story; maybe he would finish off the wounded man or mock him as he walked by.

Then came the surprise ending: the Samaritan was the hero of the story. The crowd gasped and started to mutter. Jesus posed one final question to the lawyer: "Which of these three, do you think, proved to be a neighbor to the man?" (verse 36 ESV).

Two thousand years later, there is still a bit of this lawyer in each of us, I'm afraid. We still look for ways to justify loving our good neighbors while ignoring our bad ones. I'm not just talking about the people who live on our block or in our apartment building. I mean those whose lives intersect ours regularly; people we always look at but never see, people who need help but are all too easy to ignore.

There are three typical responses when we come across a neighbor in need. Let's look briefly at each one.

It's Not My Problem

Verse 31 says, "Now by chance a priest was going down that road, and when he saw him he passed by on the other side" (ESV). Priests were representatives of the people before God. Their job was to offer sacrifices and carry out other religious duties that would bring sinful people closer to a holy God.

If anyone would have had a passion for hurting people, it should have been this priest. Apparently, though, he had more pressing matters. He had somewhere more important to be. He crossed the street, as if avoiding eye contact. After all, it's easier to ignore what you don't see. So instead of investing time and effort in helping this man, he invested his energy in avoiding him.

If we're not careful, we will walk past problems we have the answer to. We will say, "It's not my problem because it's not my fault. I didn't cause this, so I don't have to help." But just because you didn't cause a problem doesn't mean you aren't the answer to the problem.

Saying, "It's not my problem" is often an indication we are living for ourselves instead of other people. Even if the suffering we see is not something we are able to change, we should still allow our hearts to be touched and even broken by the need. Don't cross the street; that doesn't help anyone.

This man was a priest. It was his job and his calling to help people, and there was a hurt person right in front of him—but he ignored him. His behavior contradicted his title.

Is following Jesus about a title? Is the point to call ourselves "Christian," "leader," "pastor"? Or is it to love people like Jesus loves them? It's interesting that the villains in this scenario all had titles: the priest, the Levite, not to mention the lawyer himself. It was the unnamed and unknown Samaritan, though, who really deserved honor.

King Solomon, known in the Bible as the wisest man in history, once faced a dilemma. Two women claimed the same baby as their own. Obviously DNA testing was not an option, so Solomon resorted to a more extreme solution. He called for a soldier to cut the baby in half.

Here's how the Bible records what happened next:

> Then the woman who was the real mother of the living child, and who loved him very much, cried out, "Oh no, my lord! Give her the child—please do not kill him!"
>
> But the other woman said, "All right, he will be neither yours nor mine; divide him between us!"
>
> Then the king said, "Do not kill the child, but give him to the woman who wants him to live, for she is his mother!"
>
> (1 KINGS 3:26–27 NLT)

The real mom didn't care about a title. She didn't care about recognition. She cared about her baby, and she was willing to do whatever it took to save him. She had the heart of a mother, and that is far more important than the title of mother.

In the same way, following Jesus is more than a name or a label, and knowing God is more than a job. If we have truly met Jesus, the friend of sinners, we won't be able to duck our heads, cross the street, and hurry along. We will stop and engage the situation before us. We will be motivated not by a title or a job description, but by something deep within our hearts and souls: the compassion and love of Jesus for hurting people.

> Following Jesus is more than a name or a label, and knowing God is more than a job.

The Problem Is Too Big

Sometimes we avoid the first wrong response, saying it's not our problem, but fall into this response: that the problem is too big. We feel overwhelmed and underqualified to face people's problems and pain, so we walk away.

I think that is what the Levite represents in this story of the good Samaritan. Levites were usually assistants to the priests. They carried out tasks related to the temple. This Levite, when he came face-to-face with a real human struggling with real problems, might have thought, *This is too much. This is a job for a priest. Too bad there's no one around who can help this man.* And he, too, crossed the street and hurried off.

Can I be honest? Phrases like "I can't do that" or "I'm not qualified" or "I'm not ready for that" are often a mask for laziness or fear. It's easier to plead ignorance than to jump in and figure it out. I don't say that judgmentally. I've done this many times myself. But Jesus is the friend of everyone, including the Toms and Aarons in life; and if we are going to follow him, he'll lead us into scenarios for which we might feel unqualified.

Laziness lies to us and tells us someone else will fix the problem. It's a renter's mentality versus an owner's mentality. A renter's mentality says, "I'm not here for long. I'm just passing through, so what I do doesn't matter that much."

Have you ever rented a car? When I'm driving a rental, I treat it differently than my own car. The rental might be a Ford Focus, but I drive it like it's a Ferrari. I go through the drive-through at fast food restaurants, and I don't even consider cleaning out my trash. I hit speed bumps at a velocity calculated to catch air. It's not that I try to treat it differently—I just don't have any ownership in the car, so I'm not thinking long-term.

If we aren't careful, though, we can adopt a temporary, I'm-just-passing-through mentality toward people. Rather than owning our responsibility and our potential to help in each encounter, we can assume someone else will take time for them: someone better qualified, someone more experienced, someone with more time on their hands.

I Know the Answer

This third response, of course, is the correct one, and the Samaritan demonstrates it. He is the protagonist, the hero, in this story. The priest said it wasn't his problem, the Levite was overwhelmed by the size of the problem, but the Samaritan found a solution to the problem.

Ironically, the Samaritan appeared to be the least qualified of the three. I'm sure the audience would have voted him "most likely to walk on by." No one would have blamed him if he had.

But he didn't. Luke says that when the Samaritan saw the man, he felt compassion for him. Instead of running away from him, he ran toward him. He cleaned his wounds. He picked him up and put him on his own donkey. He took him to an inn. He paid for his food, lodging, and recovery. And he promised to come back through and follow up on him.

The little phrase "had compassion" (Luke 10:33 ESV) is key in this narrative. Compassion is part emotion, part love, part passion. It's a complex thing. You can't fake it, you can't define it, and you can't restrain it. Once compassion arises in our hearts, it takes on a life of its own.

To be honest, compassion can be very frustrating. You come face-to-face with a situation that you know needs to change, and your heart won't let you just walk away. But what do you do when the situation seems beyond your ability to change? How do you respond when you feel pain, even anger, at an injustice, but you feel helpless to fix it?

Many times we settle for complaining. We settle for talking about the problem, posting online about the problem, even crying about the problem. Hopefully we also pray about the problem because prayer is always appropriate.

But often we don't really *do* anything about the problem, so we live with frustrated compassion. Compassion is not meant to stay inside us—it's meant to motivate us to action. It's meant to accomplish something. It is frustration with a purpose.

Compassion causes us to focus our dedication and our resources on something until we see results.

Frustration is often an indication of calling. It shows us where we personally are supposed to invest ourselves. Do you wonder why other people seem oblivious to something that keeps you up at night? Yes, they probably need more awareness of the issue, but they may never feel what you feel. If you are the one most upset by something, maybe you are the one called to change it. Often the situation we are complaining about, the thing that bothers us the most, is exactly what we are supposed to solve.

> If you are the one most upset by something, maybe you are the one called to change it.

The Samaritan in this story is a clear example of allowing compassion to motivate us to action. He didn't overthink the problem. He didn't commission a study to determine who caused the problem. He didn't post his opinion about the problem on Facebook. He got off his donkey and got to work. This story demonstrates four simple steps to releasing compassion that I think we can apply today.

Feel: allow yourself to feel what hurt people are experiencing.
Focus: you can't do everything, but you can do something.
Fund: give your resources toward the solution.
Follow through: don't just start; follow through to the end.

This whole story came from a question the lawyer asked: "Who is my neighbor?" The Bible even gives us his motives in asking. Verse 29 says the man, who desired to "justify himself, said to Jesus, 'And who is my neighbor?'" (esv).

And Jesus responded with a story. Classic Jesus. He never did answer the question, by the way. Instead, he ended with another question, in verse 36: "Which of these three, do you think, proved to be a neighbor to the man who fell among the robbers?" (esv).

In other words, the lawyer was asking the wrong question. The question is not, "Who is my neighbor?" The question is, "Am I a good neighbor?" It's not about *who*, it's about *you*. Being a neighbor is active, not passive. The lawyer knew the law—love God, love your neighbor—but he had entirely missed the point.

Do you know what I discovered years later about my problematic neighbors? Aaron's father was an alcoholic, and he abused his son. Aaron lived in an environment of addiction, violence, and hurt. No wonder he was a bully. Tom had chronic migraines. He suffered constant pain and ringing in his ears, and any extra noise sent him through the roof. That explains the complaints about the fireworks. It doesn't excuse their actions, but it does help explain them. And it sparks compassion in me. It helps me see them not through the filters of anger or bitterness but through the filter of love. It also makes me wish I had been a better neighbor. I can only hope they were able to watch my family and me and see Jesus.

The Best Neighbor

Right about now, you might be feeling bad for how you treated some of the Aarons and Toms in your life. Or you might be thinking of someone you know currently who is hurting, and you aren't sure how to help. It is overwhelming to consider being this kind of neighbor to everyone we encounter. I don't know about you, but I don't feel like I'm up for the task. I'm still trying to learn how to love my wife; I don't know if I can love my enemies. On my best day I'm not even close to the good Samaritan.

After the lawyer recognized that the real neighbor was the Samaritan, Jesus told him, "You go, and do likewise" (verse 37 ESV). That sounds great, but ultimately, it's impossible. No one can be that good, that generous, all the time.

Jesus' audience must have been saying to each other, "This is crazy. That's what we have to do to keep the law? That's what it means to please God? This is impossible. Who could ever do that?"

Jesus probably smiled. "I know someone. Me."

Yes, it's impossible to love like that. That was Jesus' point. Ultimately, this story is not about you and me, but about Jesus. We need to be reminded of something. I've said it a dozen times already, but it's amazing how easily we overlook it: *we are not the answer.* We know the answer, but we aren't the answer. Jesus is.

Yes, we should love people. Yes, God will put people in our paths we can assist. Yes, compassion will motivate us to seek and aid people in need. We have the privilege of helping people, but we don't go to a hurting world on the basis of our own goodness, our own holiness, or our own efforts. We take Jesus to a hurting world because Jesus is the good Samaritan in this story. That is what he was trying to say. The whole story was a setup to point people to him.

Let me take it a step further. The person on the side of the road is you and me. Sin left us beat up and bleeding in a ditch.

We were hurting and helpless. We needed a Savior. Religion and law couldn't help—they just walked on by. But Jesus found us, Jesus stopped for us, and Jesus saved us. Jesus is the ultimate Good Samaritan, the best neighbor we could ever ask for.

Paul wrote in Romans 5:10, "For if, while we were God's enemies, we were reconciled to him through the death of his Son, how much more, having been reconciled, shall we be saved through his life!"

We needed a Savior just as badly as this beat-up man on the side of the road. Something changes in our hearts when we remember that. It's what I've been saying throughout this book. Jesus is the friend of sinners. He took the initiative to come to earth, to die for our sins, to reach out to us when we were unable to save ourselves.

Loving our neighbors doesn't mean trying as hard as we can to feel warm, fuzzy feelings for mean people. That doesn't work. It doesn't mean forcing ourselves to help people we'd rather put six feet under. That doesn't work either. Loving our neighbors is less about us and more about Jesus. It means being so full of God's heart for humanity and his compassion for hurting people that we naturally help them. It means that we lead them to the ultimate Good Samaritan, Jesus.

In the fourth century AD, the Roman emperor Julian resented the rise of Christianity and wanted to restore the influence of Roman pagan religions. He wrote the following about Christians:

> These impious Galileans not only feed their own poor, but ours also; welcoming them into their agape, they attract them, as children are attracted, with cakes. . . . Whilst the

pagan priests neglect the poor, the hated Galileans devote themselves to works of charity and by a display of false compassion have established and given effect to their pernicious errors. See their love-feasts and their tables spread for the indigent. Such practice is common among them and causes a contempt for our gods.[1]

How generous, how loving, and how neighborly must Christians have been to catch the attention of the emperor? It wasn't their speeches or protests that he noticed; it wasn't their doctrines; it wasn't their political stance. It was their love. Their faith was so tangible and real that people across the empire were turning to Jesus.

> **Something happens when we truly follow Jesus, the friend of sinners: we become friends of sinners.**

Something happens when we truly follow Jesus, the friend of sinners: we become friends of sinners. We become neighbors of everybody. Cultural barriers and racial prejudice find no place in our hearts because instead of trying to exclude people by asking, "Who is my neighbor?" we include everybody by asking, "How can I be a better neighbor? To whom can I be a neighbor?"

Jesus wants to bring peace and unity to a broken world. He loves the entire world, not just one nation or ethnic background. His plan to bring healing involves you and me. Our calling is to seek and save those who have been beaten up by life and left to die on the side of the proverbial road. It doesn't matter if they are different from us. It doesn't matter if they got themselves into their mess. It doesn't matter if they are "sinners," whatever that even means to you—because as we already saw, we are all sinners, so the label is a bit pointless.

We are called to be good neighbors, and we have the best neighbor, Jesus himself, as our example. I still think the song "I Love You with the Love of the Lord" was a bit creepy. But there's also a lot of truth to it. God's love is far better than our love, and his love is available for all.

Who is difficult for you to love? Is it a neighbor, a coworker, a brother-in-law, a student? Instead of forcing an empty smile, take a moment to really see them. Allow compassion to spring up in your heart. Allow yourself to see the wounds, the pain, the hopelessness. Then let Jesus' love flow through you. Let Jesus heal them. Let Jesus bring them life. You'll be amazed at what the Good Samaritan can do.

CHAPTER 9

COMFORTABLY UNCOMFORTABLE

RECENTLY I WAS DOING A BIT OF SELF-reflection, and I realized something: I love talking. I look back on my life, and I've always been a talker. I suspect a lot of people knew that before I did. I can't help it—when I'm excited about something, I want to share it. I want to convince you to be as excited about it as I am.

While we're on the topic of me—which is a bit awkward, but there's a point here, I promise—I also love new hobbies. In college, there was a period of time I was into hunting. Then I got into scuba diving. Then golf. Then cycling. Then I bought a dog, who turned out to be demon possessed, but that's another story.

I love the excitement of picking up new hobbies. Unfortunately, I think that defeats the purpose of a hobby, because a hobby is something you are supposed to do long enough to actually get good at it. I just get excited about something, try it for a couple months, and move on. I guess my hobby is getting new hobbies.

Therefore, if we meet someday, be warned: I'll immediately

start talking to you because that's what I do. And the subject of our conversation will be the greatest thing on earth that I've just discovered and you have to try because I'm sure you'll love it, too, so what are you waiting for? Except by the time you learn to love it, I will have moved on to something else.

Here's the point I promised: we tend to talk about what we are passionate about. Some personality types might use fewer superlatives and exaggerations than I do, but we all talk about our passions. It's human nature to share with other humans the things that excite us.

I think we especially love to share good news. I know I do. This has gotten me in trouble more than once because I spend a lot of time with a microphone in my hand. If I know something exciting about someone, I want to share it publicly. Recently a couple in my church got engaged. They were planning their wedding, but they were keeping it quiet because they were just going to have a small ceremony. I didn't know that. I announced from the stage how pumped I was and how cool this wedding was going to be.

Another couple told me they were going to have a baby boy. They are good friends of mine. The husband oversees our photography team, and the wife is in charge of our welcome team. I was so excited for them, and I told them I was going to tell everyone. They said, "Rich, um, it's not your news to tell."

I said, "Oh, right. I'll keep it confidential." Which we all knew meant I wouldn't use the mic and the stage to tell people, but it didn't mean I would stay totally silent.

How do you keep good news confidential? How do you keep something you are passionate about a secret? You don't! Somehow you always find a way to work it into a conversation.

Maybe you just bought a house. Your coworkers are talking about the newest gluten-free, dairy-free, joy-free diet, and you pipe up: "You know where you can cook food like that? In my new kitchen! You know, the kitchen in my *new house*. It's new! Did I say that already?"

Maybe you just found out you're going to be a parent. Nothing is going to stop you from sharing your excitement. You can be at a funeral, and you figure out how to tell people about it. You're pulling out your phone and showing strangers pictures of the ultrasound.

If you were just hired for your dream job, you tell everyone. If you just got engaged, you flash your ring everywhere you go. If you just bought a new car, you park in the most obvious parking place possible. If you go on vacation, you post pictures online to make as many people jealous as possible.

It's the irresistible, unavoidable, inexorable calling of good news. It must be expressed. It demands to be heard.

Nearly three thousand years ago, the prophet Isaiah gave the nation of Judah a message about good news. It was a prophecy predicting two events that were far in the future. First, in about a hundred years, Judah was going to be conquered by Babylon. Second, in about a thousand years, a Messiah, a Savior, would be born to save his people. Here is part of the message:

> Comfort, comfort my people,
> says your God.
> Speak tenderly to Jerusalem,
> and proclaim to her
> that her hard service has been completed,
> that her sin has been paid for,

that she has received from the LORD's hand
double for all her sins.

(ISAIAH 40:1–2)

The people listening to Isaiah had no idea what he was talking about. The prophecy didn't give many details or dates. Many decades later, though, when Babylon invaded and the nation began experiencing the heartache and judgment their sin had caused, people remembered Isaiah's message. They took comfort in his promise that a Messiah would come to rescue them, although they still didn't know whom to expect or when to expect him.

Then Jesus came to earth. It took people a while to figure it out, but, eventually, many people realized he was the promised Savior. His salvation isn't political—it's far better than that. His salvation is spiritual and eternal. Ultimately, our comfort is found in the good news, the best news, that has ever been preached: that God came to earth, died for our sins, and granted us forgiveness.

So to recap, Isaiah promised comfort, and Jesus is the fulfillment of that promise. Jesus gives us freedom from sin and guilt. He is our Savior, our Messiah, our deliverer. No matter who we are, the good news of Jesus is for us. I spent the first four chapters of this book talking about this message of grace and forgiveness Jesus brought to humanity.

That wasn't Isaiah's whole message, though. First, he promised comfort, then he gave a command. He told Judah what needed to be done with the message of God's comfort. Here are his words:

You who bring good news to Zion,

go up on a high mountain.

You who bring good news to Jerusalem,

lift up your voice with a shout,

lift it up, do not be afraid;

say to the towns of Judah,

"Here is your God!"

See, the Sovereign LORD comes with power,

and he rules with a mighty arm.

See, his reward is with him,

and his recompense accompanies him.

He tends his flock like a shepherd:

He gathers the lambs in his arms

and carries them close to his heart;

he gently leads those that have young.

(ISAIAH 40:9–11)

In other words, the good news of God's comfort and forgiveness is not meant to be confidential. It's meant to be shouted from the mountaintops and proclaimed in the streets.

Sometimes we think that we have to psych ourselves up before we share Jesus with people. We think we have to gather all our courage and prepare all our arguments. No wonder it feels artificial or forced when we do manage to talk about Jesus—it is!

Truth be told, we really just need to be passionate about Jesus. Once we experience his love and grace for ourselves, we won't have to force anything. We will naturally talk about him. We will work his love into our conversations, not because we are trying to, but because we can't help ourselves. We talk about what we are excited about, so we need to be excited about him.

Isaiah said, "Go up on a high mountain" and "lift up your voice with a shout" (verse 9). I love that picture. He is saying, "This message needs to be heard. It's important. It's a good message; it's good news."

In other words, it's not about the messenger; it's about the message. The message is so good, it must be told. The news is so amazing, we can't keep silent.

As I mentioned earlier, in the fall of 2015, our church had the opportunity to do a reality show called *Rich in Faith*, which aired on the Oxygen Network. It was a docuseries that followed my wife and me as we launched Vous Church. The experience was simultaneously challenging and incredible. It was challenging because the scrutiny of our marriage, our ministry, and our personal lives was intense; but it was incredible because we were able to reach people with the message of Jesus who might not otherwise have listened.

Someone asked me the other day, "Why on earth would you do a reality show?" Because we are supposed to take this message to the highest places, the most visible places, the most influential places of our society. I believe the gospel should influence TV. I believe it should influence music. I believe it should influence fashion, art, education, and politics.

I'm not saying we should force people to believe what we believe. I'm saying we should allow the good news to be heard, and people can make up their own minds. We live in a culture overwhelmed by bad news. Why shouldn't they hear some good news for a change?

Don't Get Comfortable

There is a big difference between being comforted and being comfortable. I've heard it said that "Jesus comforts the afflicted and afflicts the comfortable." We are meant to find comfort in Jesus, but that doesn't mean our lives will always be comfortable. The relief, peace, and joy we find in Jesus are not just for us, they are for those around us as well. If we make the Christian life just about ourselves—our comfort, our happiness, our blessings— we've missed half of Isaiah's message, and we've missed God's heart.

God loves the whole world, not just you and me. He wants to help the whole world and comfort the whole world. And for that to happen, we might need to be uncomfortable from time to time. God wants us to enjoy his comfort, but he doesn't want us to just keep it for ourselves. There is a hurting planet out there that is desperate for the good news of Jesus and the comfort he brings. We are the news carriers. We are the gospel proclaimers. We are the heralds, and Jesus is the message.

Jesus is the best example of this. He left the comforts of heaven and was born in a stable. That's the most extreme riches-to-rags story ever. Then he died on a cross, one of the most gruesome, painful deaths imaginable. He gave it all up so you and I could find hope again. He made himself uncomfortable so we could be comforted. How could we do otherwise?

If we have been comforted by God, we should be willing to be uncomfortable for him. Jesus had no problem talking this way with his disciples. He said things like, "Whoever wants to be my disciple must deny themselves and take up their cross and follow me" (Matthew 16:24). That sounds slightly uncomfortable.

On another occasion he said, "I am sending you out like sheep among wolves" (Matthew 10:16). I read that and think, *Don't wolves eat sheep? Jesus, was that the most encouraging metaphor you could think of?*

During his last moments on earth, he told his disciples, "Therefore go and make disciples of all nations" (Matthew 28:19). Again, his point is clear. We are not called to sit around congratulating each other on our future in heaven. There is a mandate to tell others about the comfort and hope found in Jesus.

This principle of taking in and giving out is as natural as breathing. How long can you hold your breath? A few seconds? A minute? Two minutes, if you're Michael Phelps or a mutant? Holding on to one breath gets really uncomfortable, really fast. We were designed to inhale, then exhale, then inhale again. In the same way, we receive comfort, then we give comfort, then we continue to receive comfort. It's a rhythm and a cycle inherent to life.

Sometimes as followers of Jesus, we get more obsessed with receiving than with giving. When we get the order mixed up, life gets mixed up. It's not about getting, it's about giving. There is a rhythm to it.

I was at the airport the other day—no surprise there—and I was on a train that shuttles passengers between terminals. I came to my stop, and the doors opened. A group of us were about to get off, but there was a family of maybe ten people, all carrying their bags, that tried to get on as soon as the doors opened. They didn't adhere to the proper rhythm and flow. They insisted on pushing ahead when they should have yielded, and it created a completely unnecessary traffic jam.

There is a God-created rhythm to life. You can see it in

nature, in the way seeds become trees and trees produce seeds; in the way babies grow up and have more babies; in the way stars are born and explode and create more stars—or turn into black holes and destroy everything in their vicinity, in some cases. But you know what I mean.

As you embrace the rhythm of receiving and giving, you discover God has more in store for you. God fills you up in order to spill you out.

Why do you come to church? To get filled up.

Why do you read your Bible? To get filled up.

Why do you worship? To get filled up.

Why do you take time to pray? To get filled up.

Why get filled up, though? Just to be really full, really comfortable Christians? No! You and I get filled up so we have enough for others as well, so we can be spilled out for others, so we can get uncomfortable for others.

Proverbs 11:25 says, "A generous person will prosper; whoever refreshes others will be refreshed." Our society and culture tell us the opposite: if you get uncomfortable for someone, you'll lose something. You'll be hurt. You'll regret it.

God says if you help someone, he will help you. If you bless someone, he will bless you. If you get uncomfortable for someone, he will bring you comfort. If you refresh someone, he will make sure you get refreshed because that's how the cycle works.

Paul understood this principle. He told the Corinthian believers:

Praise be to the God and Father of our Lord Jesus Christ, the Father of compassion and the God of all comfort, who comforts us in all our troubles, so that we can comfort those in any trouble with the comfort we ourselves receive from God. For just as we share abundantly in the sufferings of Christ, so also our comfort abounds through Christ. If we are distressed, it is for your comfort and salvation; if we are comforted, it is for your comfort, which produces in you patient endurance of the same sufferings we suffer. And our hope for you is firm, because we know that just as you share in our sufferings, so also you share in our comfort.

(2 CORINTHIANS 1:3–7)

I count the word *comfort* nine times in five verses. Paul made it very clear: God comforts us so we can comfort others, and for us to comfort others, we might need to get uncomfortable.

> God comforts us so we can comfort others, and for us to comfort others, we might need to get uncomfortable.

We need to get comfortable with being uncomfortable. We need to learn how to be uncomfortable while maintaining a spirit of comfort. In other words, we need to keep the flow going with God. He comforts us, heals us, guides us, and refreshes us; and we turn around and pour that out to others.

Why is it hard for us to step outside of our comfort zones and help others? I'm sure each of us has different reasons, but here are three things I've observed that we need to overcome.

Overcome Fear

There's no shame in experiencing fear from time to time. Fear is a natural emotion meant to protect us. It alerts us to danger and reminds us to be cautious and wise in potentially risky situations. Fear becomes a negative, however, when we allow it to influence us more than it should.

Leaving our comfort zones is scary. That's what "comfort zone" means, after all—it's the areas or situations where we feel confident, secure, in control. That means everything outside that comfort zone is, by definition, the *uncomfortable* zone. It's uncharted territory. It's not that certain death awaits us out there—but it might. Who knows? Who can tell? We've never been there, so maybe there is reason to be afraid. That fear of the unknown is enough to hold many people back.

Let's be honest, though. Fear of the unknown hasn't gotten anyone anywhere. What if Abraham Lincoln had been afraid of how our country would fare after slavery was abolished? What if Lewis and Clark had been afraid of the uncharted West? What if Neil Armstrong had been afraid of the unknown that awaited him on the moon? They probably *were* afraid—but they didn't let that stop them, and history will forever remember their names.

We must step past the limits our fears impose. Imagine if Neil Armstrong had stayed in the landing capsule. "Houston, we have a problem. I don't know what's out there, and frankly, I'm a bit nervous about it. I'd like to go home now. Abort mission. Hey, do we have a latte machine in this thing?"

That would have been ridiculous. Instead, he strapped on

his air pack and stepped into the unknown void, saying, "That's one small step for man, one giant leap for mankind." In other words, it was a small step that felt huge. Physically, the distance wasn't much, but emotionally and psychologically, it was enormous.

That's where some of us are when it comes to talking about Jesus with friends and coworkers. We need to take a little step, but it feels so big. Can I encourage you? Once you take the step the first time, it will never feel so big again. Your comfort zone will simply expand.

Some of us don't talk to people about Jesus because we wonder, *What if I say the wrong thing?* Jesus told his disciples, "When you are arrested, don't worry about how to respond or what to say. God will give you the right words at the right time. For it is not you who will be speaking—it will be the Spirit of your Father speaking through you" (Matthew 10:19–20 NLT).

In the context, Jesus was referring to religious persecution. Most of us don't face that too often, at least not to the point of being thrown in prison. The principle is the same, though: we don't need to fear intimidating circumstances or antagonistic people because God will help us say the right thing.

Starting Vous Church was a simultaneously exhilarating and terrifying experience for DawnCheré and me and for our team. We went so far away from our comfort zone we forgot where our comfort zone was. Everything was new; everything was risky; everything was uncharted.

One of the most exciting—and intimidating—opportunities we had was to be interviewed by several major TV networks. I'm not sure why these media outlets felt Vous Church might make a good story; maybe because of the reality show or my previous book or my reputation as a speaker. Regardless, we were thrilled at the opportunity to shine a light on Jesus and talk about him through national media channels, but the responsibility to accurately portray Jesus and Christianity weighed on our minds and emotions.

The day we launched our church, ABC's *Nightline* came and covered the opening. Just starting a church is scary enough. But having a reporter with a mic in your face the whole time saying, "How's it going, Rich? What are you thinking?" adds another layer of scary.

As I was getting ready for a forty-five-minute interview I had to do that night, I remember feeling so nervous. I called my friend Shawn, and I said, "I don't know if I can do this." I wasn't afraid of talking about God, but I was afraid of misrepresenting him, of misrepresenting Christianity.

God gave me the words to say that night. I'm not saying it was perfect or that no one criticized us. There are always critics. But it turned out to be an incredibly exciting experience, and I was able to proclaim the good news from another mountaintop in our culture.

Time and time again, I find myself in spaces where I wonder if I'm setting myself up to be ridiculed, if I'm setting myself up to be criticized, if I'm setting myself up to drop the ball. But every time I have gotten into one of those spaces, God's grace has shown up. When I didn't have the words to say, God gave me the words.

Again, it's about the message, not the messenger. It's been said that God doesn't call the qualified, he qualifies the called. Sometimes you just have to say, "Okay, here I go. I'm not qualified, but there's no one else to do this. God, this is on you!"

It's the process, it's the rhythm. Inhale, exhale. Be filled up, be spilled out. We were created for this.

Isaiah specifically addressed fear in his message. Verse 9 of Isaiah 40 says, "You who bring good news to Jerusalem, lift up your voice with a shout, lift it up, do not be afraid."

There are several ways to deal with fear. Some people run away from fear; they look for an escape, a distraction, a way out. Other people carry fear; they live burdened and stressed by what might happen in the future. But the best way to deal with fear, and in the long run the easiest way, is to face it. It's to recognize the reality of the threat and determine to press on anyway. When you face fear, God gives you the grace to walk through it.

I mentioned this earlier, but it's worth repeating: when we are passionate about something, we talk about it. I've found that fear takes a backseat to passion every time. When we get excited about how good God is, when we recognize Jesus is the friend of sinners, when we remember how he has changed our lives, fears dissipate and timidity dissolves. Our passion to talk about what God has done takes over.

Overcome Shame

Maybe fear isn't holding you back, but embarrassment is. Maybe you know people are hurting, you know Jesus is the answer, and you want to help. But you don't want to impose your beliefs on people, and you don't want to be one of "those" Christians who comes across as a holier-than-thou fanatic. You are afraid people will lump you in with extremists and doomsayers if they hear you talking about Jesus.

I can understand that. There are some people out there who seem to think their beliefs give them a right to shame people, reject people, and offend people, and they do it in the name of Jesus. I'm not their judge, but I don't see Jesus living that way, and I don't read in the Bible that he asked us to live that way either.

I don't think sharing our faith means we have to be rude. We are simply called to share our hope with people as God opens doors, and then see what God does.

Unfortunately, Christians often think they can either be normal people or radical believers, but not both. So, many people choose to stay silent so they don't stand out, while others get almost militant with their faith.

Look at Jesus, though. He was normal enough that children liked to hang out with him and sinners invited him to dinner. Yet he was radical enough to change the course of history. Why do we think we have to pick one or the other? Somehow Jesus was radically normal. When it comes to following Jesus and sharing Jesus, radical needs to be the new normal, and normal needs to be the new radical.

We live in the real world, not a bubble; we need to be real people, not some subculture that never interacts with "normal" humanity. Sometimes even our conversation reflects a bubble mentality: "Hey, brother, are you blessed today? Are you covered by the blood of the Lamb?" Do we even know what that means? Even if *we* do, how about everyone else? I'm sure there's a better way to say that. Like maybe, "Bro! How are you?"

We live in real cities and real towns; we work at real jobs, go to real schools, and live in real neighborhoods. Let's be real, and part of being real is allowing the most important news we've ever heard or experienced to color our conversation and influence our actions.

Sometimes the shame isn't because we are worried about what people might think but because of something negative in our past or present. Maybe it's a failed marriage, a hidden addiction, or a secret sin that haunts our hearts and sabotages us with shame. God fills us up with his grace, but somehow we think it's not enough. Our mistakes, our addictions, our hidden flaws loom larger in our eyes than the forgiveness of God.

God doesn't just forgive us, though. He takes what the enemy meant for evil and uses it for good. Our failures can actually help us reach people better. I'm not excusing sin, but I am saying it's not fatal. Not anymore. Not since Jesus took care of it on the cross. Our weaknesses plus Jesus' grace are the perfect platform to show people what God can do in their lives as well.

> Our weaknesses plus Jesus' grace are the perfect platform to show people what God can do in their lives as well.

You'd be surprised how many people relate to your weaknesses more quickly than your strengths. They are often more impacted by God's grace showcased in your failures than by your impressive but (in their eyes) unattainable holiness. Again, that's not justification to go out and do something stupid just to relate to people. That's not even logical, considering the pain and destruction sin causes. But your mistakes are not a valid reason to stay silent about Jesus. If anything, they are the stage you stand on and speak from.

The apostle Paul wrote, "For I am not ashamed of the gospel, because it is the power of God that brings salvation to everyone who believes" (Romans 1:16). Later he told his disciple Timothy, "Never be ashamed to tell others about our Lord" (2 Timothy 1:8 NLT). Jesus is the best news imaginable. While many people might not believe that or understand that, the fact that we believe is no cause for shame.

Sometimes we aren't ashamed of how bad we are—we are ashamed of how good we are. We feel like our lifestyle and morals separate us from others. People do notice that, of course, but I don't think the divide is as big as we think. If anything, many people wish they could share our convictions, but they don't know how.

I've heard Christians say things like, "I can't share Jesus because I don't have a good testimony. I grew up in the church. I never did drugs. I never slept around. What do I have to tell people?"

That's crazy. There is no such thing as a bad testimony or a good testimony. There are just testimonies. The word *testimony* simply means affirming that something is true. Revelation 12:11 talks about people who overcame "by the blood of the Lamb and by the word of their testimony." Your testimony is your story of Jesus. It's your personal experience, your observation of what it's like to know Jesus.

Your testimony doesn't have to be dramatic: "God healed me from cancer," or "God set me free from alcoholism." Those epic miracles are awesome and faith-inspiring, but often the story that resonates the most with people is, "God comforted me. God loved me. God gave me peace." Those are needs everyone faces; therefore, they are often the best points of connection.

A person with an experience will always have more to say than a person with an argument. How can someone argue with an experience? Your story is your story, and no one can take that away. Don't be ashamed to share it. As Paul wrote, people will be comforted by hearing about the comfort you received in God.

Overcome Apathy

Some people don't struggle with fear or shame, but they do struggle with apathy. Actually, they probably don't struggle with it, because apathy by definition means not caring. So they just give in to their apathy.

Apathy can be defined as "passion removed." It means indifference, coldness, lack of feeling about something. I started this chapter talking about passion, so I've come full circle here.

Without a passion for Jesus, you won't be motivated to share about him with others. Passion is a product of knowledge and experience. The more you know Jesus, the more you understand what he's done for you, and the more you realize how much he can do for hurting people around you, the more motivated you will be to make yourself uncomfortable so others can be comforted.

There was a photographer named Kevin Carter who went to the Sudan in 1993 to document the war and famine taking place there. The horrors he witnessed were unimaginable, but his photographs helped bring awareness in other nations and spur people to action.

On one occasion Carter came across a tiny child on the

brink of starvation. The child was emaciated, whimpering, attempting to crawl toward a feeding center. Suddenly a vulture landed nearby. The photographer had been told not to touch victims because of the threat of disease, so he simply took photographs of the heart-wrenching scene. Finally he scared the bird off and watched as the child crawled toward the center. Then he lit a cigarette, prayed, and wept.

The *New York Times* ran the photo. Readers around the world wrote and called, asking what happened to the child. Carter had to reply that he did not know. He didn't pick up the child. He didn't carry the child to safety. He simply watched from the sidelines.

Carter won a Pulitzer Prize for the photo. It became an iconic image of the horrors of the Sudan famine. But the darkness of that moment and others like it never left him. He committed suicide three months after winning the Pulitzer Prize. He wrote, "I am haunted by the vivid memories of killings & corpses & anger & pain."[1]

Carter brought awareness to the problem, but not aid. I can't criticize him. We've all been guilty of watching from a distance and not doing anything. At least Carter was on the front lines. At least he was invested and aware. But it wasn't enough, and it haunted him.

I don't want to be known as the generation that brings awareness but not solutions. We are in danger of becoming the generation that Instagrams about issues, that tweets about travesties, but that does nothing personally to change them. Are we reporters or rescuers? Are we activists or slacktivists? Will we set down the camera, pick the child up, and save a life? I'm not referring just to political or social issues, although those are important. I'm talking about our relationship to the world at large. Will we step up and assume our responsibility as Jesus followers to help people in whatever capacity we can?

I am grateful that God is not apathetic. Really, that's the point of this book. That's what I mean by "friend of sinners." God isn't passively observing the plight of humanity. He is actively involved. He sent his Son to die for us. He hears our prayers. He gives us aid. He is preparing a place for us. And one day he will return to take us to heaven.

> **God isn't passively observing the plight of humanity. He is actively involved.**

The book of Isaiah has been called a Bible in miniature. It has sixty-six chapters. The first thirty-nine chapters are primarily about judgment, but starting in chapter 40, the focus turns to the comfort and salvation found in the coming Messiah. Similarly, the Bible has sixty-six books. The first thirty-nine, the Old Testament, focus on the law and God's mercy. Then, starting with the birth of Jesus, the New Testament focuses on the fulfillment of that law and on salvation through the blood of Jesus. Jesus is the Messiah, the promised comforter, whom God has sent for our salvation.

Look again at what Isaiah wrote in 40:11:

> He tends his flock like a shepherd:
> He gathers the lambs in his arms
> and carries them close to his heart;
> he gently leads those that have young.

God's love and concern for humanity are clear. He longs to carry and comfort hurting individuals. Why are we passionate about people? Because God is passionate about people and because God is passionate about *us*.

Will you consider making yourself uncomfortable to bring comfort to others? Will you allow God to replace fear, shame, or apathy with his passion for people? I promise you, the reward is worth the risk. You have answers; you have hope; you have healing. It's time to share it with the world.

CHAPTER 10

HOW TO BE GREAT

HAVE YOU EVER NOTICED WE ALL WANT
to be great? We might have different definitions of greatness,
and we might have different goals and dreams, but none of us
wants to be average or second best. We want to be important.
We want our lives to matter.

The search for greatness is a normal part of human existence.
When you go shopping, you don't look for average clothes. You
look for the best: best fashion, best value, best quality. When
you eat at a restaurant, you don't ask the server, "Could you
recommend a really average dish? I'm in the mood for something kind of blah." You ask which dish is the best because you
want an amazing dining experience. When you go to a movie,
you don't look up reviews and find the most mediocre film
available. You look for the movie the critics are raving about and
people love. We look for the best we can get because we desire
greatness.

I grew up as a preacher's kid, as I mentioned earlier. My
father is my hero, but he's one of those scary preachers. He has

a heart of gold, but he has eyes that see into your soul. When he looks at you, it's like he can tell what you did Friday night.

When I was growing up in Tacoma, Washington, my dad was a well-known figure in the town. He wasn't just known for his preaching, though. He was also known for being absolutely passionate at his kids' sports events. It was as if he turned into another person. A hidden side of his personality would burst through, like Dr. Jekyll and Mr. Hyde. He was "that parent," the one that out-cheered (or out-yelled, depending on the score) every other parent.

I remember one particular basketball game. I think I was in seventh grade, and I was on the junior varsity squad. I was having a terrible game. I was missing shots and rebounds, and I kept getting called for fouls. I racked up four fouls, one away from fouling out. I could tell just by glancing at my dad he was about to lose it.

Then it happened. I tried to block a shot, and the ref blew his whistle and signaled a foul against me. That was when my dad lost it. It was like righteous anger started to come all over him. I didn't know if it was the spirit of God or something else—it was hard to tell.

"*Ref!*" he yelled. "Are you *blind*? That was a horrible call! You're a terrible referee." Everyone in the stands looked at my dad. They all heard him clearly. And so did the referee.

I'll never forget what happened next. It was burned into my adolescent brain. The referee looked at my dad and yelled, "Pastor! You're outta here!" My dad, Reverend Wilkerson, was ejected from the game.

I was embarrassed, but it was also kind of awesome. I remember thinking, *Why does my dad care this much? Why does he get so passionate about a seventh-grade JV game?*

I discovered the answer a couple years ago. I was back in Washington State visiting my older brother, Jonfulton. He has a daughter named Israel, who was two years old at the time.

One afternoon Jonfulton asked me, "Rich, do you want to go with me to Israel's swim lesson?"

"Absolutely," I said.

We got to the swim lesson, and Israel got in the water with about fifteen other kids. All of a sudden something came over me. It was the same spirit that hit my dad. I began to freak out. I yelled, "Come on, Israel! You can do it! You are God's chosen one. You're the next Olympic champion!"

My brother looked at me and said, "Rich, what's wrong with you? This is just a swim lesson."

I said, "Swim lesson? Come on, man! She's in the water, and there are other kids. This is a race, and she has to be first. She has to be the best. She has to be great!" In the middle of flipping out, it hit me: *I've become my father.*

Whether we admit it or not, down deep, we all want to be in first place. We all want to be great. Even in our walk with God and our spiritual journey, none of us prays, "God, make me average."

The problem, though, is often we don't know the correct path to greatness. We try to achieve greatness the wrong way.

This isn't just a twenty-first-century problem. Even Jesus' disciples had wrong ideas about greatness. The gospel of Mark records a conversation where Jesus addressed their quest to be great, and what he told them can teach us a lot today.

They came to Capernaum. When he was in the house, he asked them, "What were you arguing about on the road?"

But they kept quiet because on the way they had argued about who was the greatest.

Sitting down, Jesus called the Twelve and said, "Anyone who wants to be first must be the very last, and the servant of all."

He took a little child whom he placed among them. Taking the child in his arms, he said to them, "Whoever welcomes one of these little children in my name welcomes me; and whoever welcomes me does not welcome me but the one who sent me."

(9:33–37)

Road Trips

Jesus and his disciples were on a road trip. Road trips, especially when the car is full, are both awesome and agonizing. They have a unique effect on your psyche. If you ever took trips like these as a kid, you can probably relate. We did a lot of them, always in the stereotypical minivan, and I'm still scarred.

Being in close proximity to the same people for extended periods of time tends to reveal immaturities and insecurities you didn't know you had. The trip always starts out great—you have plenty of snacks, someone puts on a cool playlist, the windows are down, and the vibe is amazing. What could go wrong?

About five hundred miles, that's what goes wrong. Sometime in the middle of nowhere, when the AC isn't working, you haven't slept well, and you haven't been able to find a bathroom for hours, fallen human nature makes an appearance. It starts with impatience and complaints.

"Are we there yet?"

"No!"

"How much farther?"

"Hours. Lots of hours. Stop asking."

When you realize the trip is nowhere close to over, your attention turns from the road outside to the company inside. You start to argue with your siblings. You get irritated at your friends. You wonder whose idea it was to take this road trip from hell.

But then, eventually, you make it to some sliver of civilization. You fill your tank and stomach, empty your bladder, and the trip becomes fun again. Then the cycle repeats.

That's more or less the situation with the disciples. Somewhere along the hot, dusty road, they got into an argument about who was the greatest. Maybe it started with Simon the Zealot taking offense at some random comment by Peter the Loudmouth, then people took sides, and the whole thing escalated into a clash of opinions and personalities. From there, everyone started talking about themselves: the people they had helped, the miracles they had done, the time they had spent with Jesus, and so on, trying to prove how important they were.

It's easy to criticize these twelve guys, but we do the same thing on our spiritual journey. The road is long, the process is arduous, and at some point we start to ask God, "Are we there yet? How much farther until I reach my destiny? When will I find significance and recognition? When will I be great?"

We want immediate greatness, but we don't want the process. And yet greatness is more about the journey than the destination, and it's more about the people you are traveling with than the place you are traveling to.

You don't arrive at greatness, by the way. It's not some tangible, measurable goal: a six-figure salary, a million Twitter followers, a house on the beach. Greatness is who you are, not what you do, and the journey is what polishes and perfects that within us.

We are on a journey with Jesus. It's a lifelong journey, and it will have high moments and low moments. We tend to be so enamored by the highlights. We love ESPN because it just shows us the highlights, the best moments. They never show the hours of practice, yet it's the hours in anonymity that produce those seconds in the spotlight. Our road trip with Jesus is not about the highlights; it's about his presence in the process. That is more important than where we've been or what we've done.

In the journey of life, we don't just complain about "not being there yet." We also tend to argue with other people about petty things. We want our voices to be heard, our feelings to be validated, our opinions to be respected.

Can we all agree the disciples' debate over greatness was a bit ridiculous, considering the context? The disciples had Jesus at their side. Jesus is the Messiah, the Alpha and Omega, the beginning and the end, the Author and Finisher of their faith, the King of kings. I could go on, but you get the point. Yet they were bickering about which of them was the greatest. In comparison to Jesus, it was a moot point.

Christians are notorious for arguing over dumb things. For getting frustrated over things Jesus never got frustrated over. For spending time on things Jesus never spent time on. For getting offended about things Jesus never got offended about.

We are on a journey; we have Jesus in our car. He is the hero of heroes, the legend of legends. He breathed stars into existence. Can you do that? And yet we look at each other and start discussing who is the greatest. "What do you do? Where do you go on vacation? What car do you drive? What's your ministry? How big is your church? How important are you to God?" We get lost in labels and categories that are meaningless in comparison to Jesus.

A pastor came up to me at a conference not too long ago. He was really concerned. He said, "Rich, what does Vous Church believe about the end times?"

I said, "What do you mean? We believe Jesus is coming back."

He said, "Yes, but what do you believe about the rapture? Are you pre-tribulation, mid-tribulation, or post-tribulation?"

I didn't know how to reply. I didn't want to hurt his feelings, but I was not interested in where this conversation was going. There is little benefit in arguing over the chronology of events that we don't really understand and haven't happened yet. I would rather talk about how Jesus came to seek, befriend, and save sinners. I'd rather talk about God's grace and love. I'd rather work together to reach our cities for Jesus. That excites me far more than debating the beasts of the Apocalypse. Why do we care so much that our opinions be heard? That people agree we are right?

I find that focusing on Jesus keeps my ego in check. The disciples veered from that, and their arguing about greatness was ridiculous. It was then, and it is now. Striving and competing to be great in the eyes of others is pointless because we have Jesus with us. We need to keep our eyes on him. His presence, his love, and his grace are far more important than our egos.

When I am tempted to compare myself to others, to

compete with others, or to let insecurity rise in my heart, the best antidote is to look to Jesus. The greatness Jesus modeled puts our lives and desires in perspective.

It's Good to Be Great

Jesus didn't interfere. He let them argue and bicker along the way, but when they got to Capernaum, he called them together for a little chat.

It's important to note Jesus did not criticize their desire for greatness. He did not rebuke them for wanting to be great. That is significant because sometimes we think our desire for greatness is wrong in itself; that it is prideful, selfish, or superficial.

We desire greatness because we were created for greatness. It's a God-given desire, not a sinful desire. It's inherent in humanity, as I said earlier. God put within us an impulse to be the best we can be and to achieve the most we can achieve. We were designed to reach our potential. We were created in the image of a God who is great, so it's logical to sense greatness within ourselves.

> We were created in the image of a God who is great, so it's logical to sense greatness within ourselves.

Jesus didn't criticize their desire to be great. Rather, he completely redefined the pathway to greatness. It's not wrong to be great, but it's wrong to try to be great the wrong way.

The disciples—and many of us—were confused about the pathway to greatness. That is understandable because we live in a fallen, confused world. Sin has entered the equation, and the enemy, the devil, seeks to steal, kill, and destroy all that is good. He isn't a creator—he's a destroyer. So all he can do to derail God-given desires is manipulate the pathway to fulfill them. Our positive, healthy desire for greatness can be twisted into something that hurts us and others if we don't understand God's definition of greatness and his path to achieve it.

How do we define being great? What does it mean, and how do we achieve it? I see two frequent misconceptions we need to correct.

Tell Me I'm Great

It's not wrong to want to be great. The problem arises when we want to be known as great. We think *greatness means being known as great*. That's the first misconception we need to debunk.

We tend to think our greatness is connected to who recognizes us, who congratulates us, who thanks us. We fall victim to the approval of others. We believe that unless we are popular or noticed, we aren't doing anything great. We find ourselves striving, discontented, looking for peace.

Instead of thinking, *I want to be the best I can be*, we start to think, *I need people to know how great I am*. The more known we are, the greater we think we are. That's why we are obsessed with Instagram. Who liked my photo? How many followers do I have? Who knows me?

In Vous Church, we started to run into a problem. We couldn't find enough volunteers to staff the parking lot. We had lots of people who wanted to help in different areas, but no one was excited about the parking lot. Why? Because there is no glory in the parking lot. It's hot in the parking lot. You get yelled at in the parking lot. Demons manifest in the parking lot. People flip you off in the parking lot. Nobody knows your name, nobody recognizes you, nobody thanks you; they either ignore you or try to run you over.

There is never a shortage of people willing to serve on stage, but the real test of a servant heart is whether you can serve when no one knows you. If serving in obscurity is beneath you, leadership in public is beyond you.

> **You may never receive the recognition you deserve on earth, but the God of heaven knows you, loves you, and believes in you.**

Greatness is not about who knows you. You can't live your life for other people. You live for an audience of one, and his name is Jesus Christ. You may never receive the recognition you deserve on earth, but the God of heaven knows you, loves you, and believes in you.

I'm Greater Than You

The second misconception is that *greatness means being better than everyone around us.* Instead of running our own race, we look to the left and the right. As long as we're ahead of those close by, we think we're great. It's the comparison trap. We make greatness relative: it's conditional based on the performance of other people.

The problem is, you might be the best some of the time, but you won't be the best all the time. When you make other people your standard, you set yourself up for failure. It's not sustainable, it's not objective, and it's not healthy.

Comparison is a thief. It steals your contentment and your motivation. Comparison works like a scoreboard: when we do good, we think God loves and accepts us more; when we do bad, we think he loves us less. So we are constantly sizing ourselves and other people up, trying to be better than others in God's eyes.

> Comparison is a thief. It steals your contentment and your motivation.

That's not how God thinks, though, and it's not how grace works. We are already accepted and loved and called, and nothing can change that.

We each have our own lives to live, our own races to run. God doesn't give us grace to do what other people are called to do, and if we try to run their race, we will only frustrate ourselves. If you feel paralyzed in life, maybe you are more focused on the runners around you than on the race before you.

There is a story in the Bible about a shepherd boy named David who became the most famous king in Hebrew history. One time, before he was king, he tried to wear Saul's armor in a one-on-one battle against an invading army's champion soldier, a giant named Goliath. The armor wasn't designed for David, though, and it didn't fit him. He couldn't even move while he was wearing it. The thing meant to protect him ended up paralyzing him. He ended up taking it off and facing the giant with nothing but the sling and stones he was used to using as a shepherd—and he won a resounding victory. David wasn't supposed to face his battles the same way others around him faced theirs. He had his own abilities, his own path, his own wins to pursue.

Comparison is the enemy of progress. It's a recipe for pride, mediocrity, and frustration. Life isn't about beating other people. It's about being the best we can be. We need a vision from God of who we are and what we can accomplish, and then we need to run our own race, fixing our eyes only on Jesus.

Last Is the New First

The disciples were arguing about greatness, but what they really wanted was a purpose. That's what our arguments and striving usually come down to: we are trying to find our place, our calling, our role. Our real need isn't prominence, it's significance.

Jesus understood something his twelve followers needed to know: their purpose was found in how they related to other people. They would find the greatness they were looking for not by being known as great or by being greater than others but by serving others.

Remember, Jesus was the friend of sinners. That was what motivated him; that was what excited him. He wanted his disciples to understand the connection between greatness and love. They needed to see that true greatness is always about other people. Once we meet the friend of sinners, we are called to be friends of sinners. And the best way to be a friend is to serve.

He told them, "Anyone who wants to be first must be the

very last, and the servant of all" (Mark 9:35). Jesus was saying that in God's economy, last is the new first. The way up is down. The way to the top is to be at the bottom. The servant is the leader, and the leader is the servant. It's the paradox of the gospel: if you want to be first, you have to be willing to be last.

I've always loved the phrase "There's room at the bottom." Maybe you think, *There's too much competition around me. I feel like I'm bumping into people. Nobody knows what I'm doing. I can't seem to get myself out there, to get ahead, to catch a break.* Trust me, there's plenty of room at the bottom. If your goal is to serve, to love, and to help, there is more than enough opportunity for you. You will always have a place because few people think like that.

The last become first because God's ways are not the world's ways. For a while, the people who push and fight, who promote themselves, who step on the little guy to get ahead, might seem to be way ahead of the pack. But Jesus has a way of inverting everything. At some point we realize the people who seemed to be making such great progress are going in the wrong direction. God is going in a different direction; he has different priorities and a different path. Sooner or later, the people who appeared to be at the back, the people who served and gave and loved, end up with what everyone wanted all along: significance, fulfillment, value, peace.

When we understand we are called to serve others, we discover purpose and significance.

Instead of focusing on seizing opportunities, we focus on serving people.

Instead of looking for what we can get, we look for who we can help.

Instead of holding on to our lives, we give them up, knowing the God we have entrusted everything to is faithful.

Instead of finding contentment in accomplishments or titles, we find it in a person—in Jesus—and in serving the people he loves.

When we embrace service, even our pain starts to make sense. We realize our wounds can become someone else's wisdom; our hurts can become someone else's healing; our breakdown can become someone else's breakthrough.

If we want to be great, we have to be willing to be the least. We have to be willing to be unknown. That is hard to do, because fame and accolades are exciting. They appeal to our pride, they stroke our egos, and they prop up our insecurities. But, ultimately, they are a fickle friend and a false hope.

> **True greatness is not measured by who knows our name or who we're ahead of. It's measured by the impact we have on the lives of others.**

True greatness is not measured by who knows our name or who we're ahead of. It's measured by the impact we have on the lives of others. Greatness is about giving, not receiving. It's about others, not us.

What's great about greatness is that it is accessible to everyone. If greatness meant being known or being the best, then only a few people could achieve it. But if greatness is the result of service, then greatness is within all of us. Dr. Martin Luther King Jr. summed it up perfectly when he said, "Everybody can be great, because anybody can serve."

Servant leadership is our calling and identity as Jesus followers. Jesus said this about himself: "For even the Son of Man came not to be served, but to serve others, and to give his life as a ransom for many" (Mark 10:45).

Jesus used an object lesson to make his point about servant leadership clear to his disciples. He called a child over to the group and sat him down. He said, "Anyone who welcomes a little child like this on my behalf welcomes me, and anyone who welcomes me welcomes not only me but also my Father who sent me" (Mark 9:37 NLT).

What was he saying? That if they wanted to be great, they had to welcome children. They had to serve children. Until they welcomed a child, they hadn't truly welcomed Jesus.

Recently I was studying and writing by the pool. Don't hate me, that's how we do it in Miami. Best city in the world.

While I studied, I couldn't help but notice a father who had his three small boys with him at the pool. The oldest boy was maybe four years old, and the other two were twins and were about three. None of the boys knew how to swim. The guy had his hands full, to put it mildly. He seemed stressed out.

When it was time for them to go, I could tell he was bracing himself for a long ordeal. He started with the oldest. "Cody, time to get out of the pool."

"No, Dad! I want to swim!"

"No, time to get out. Come on, bud. Over here. One . . . two . . ."

So Cody climbed out, not happy at all about the situation. His dad took him to a chair, wrapped him in a towel, and told him to stay there. I could see the dad checking the kids off in his mind. *One down, two to go.*

He called the next kid. "Tommy, time to get out."

"But, Dad," Tommy said, "I want to keep swimming!"

Right then Cody zipped past his dad. He had a toy in his hand, and he threw it as far out as he could into the pool and looked like he was about to jump in after it.

"Cody, you don't know how to swim!" The dad grabbed him. "Get back from the edge. Go sit down." He turned back to the pool. "Tommy. Out. Now."

Tommy got out, also unhappy.

"Okay, Tommy, go sit with Cody over there on the cha— Cody? Get back to that chair, Cody. Tommy, sit with Cody." They both sat down. *Two down, one to go.*

He called to the last child. "Zach, come on, get out of the water. Tommy, stop! Cody, sit down! Zach, come on, I said. Tommy, sit there! Cody, put your swimsuit back on. We're in public. Zach, *now!*"

The dad had to use both arms and legs to corral all three kids. The whole ordeal lasted twenty-five minutes. I probably should have prayed for him or at least shouted encouragement, but I was too fascinated. And terrified. Eventually he got them wrapped in towels and out of the gate.

Something hit me while I watched them: that father saved his kids' lives at least seventeen times. He protected them, saved them, and served them. And they never said, "Thank you." Not even once. Actually, it was the opposite. They got mad. They threw fits. They tossed their toys back in the pool just to be obnoxious. They disobeyed.

I believe Jesus pulled a child into the story to give the disciples—and us—a practical illustration of servant leadership. A child can't repay you. A child won't thank you. A child will never mention you on Instagram. A child can't help you back. Many times when you serve a child, he or she resists it.

What was Jesus saying? That true greatness comes from serving people who will never notice, never thank you, never honor you, never give anything back. They might resist you and criticize you. They might get mad at you.

As I sat by that pool, though, I felt the Holy Spirit speak to me. "Rich, that's what you look like sometimes. You are like those boys." I started to think, how many times have I run back to the pool, determined and desperate to do my own will? How many times has Jesus rescued me, protected me, helped me? And I don't usually say thank you. If anything, I resist his limits and resent his commands.

Isn't that the picture of the gospel? Jesus loved us and died for us when we were still his enemies. He is the friend of sinners and the servant of sinners.

Jesus isn't asking us to do something he hasn't done. He is the greatest person to have ever lived, yet he is the servant of all. Now he is calling us to serve those he loves so much. He is calling us to help those who might resist our help, might resent us, and will probably never repay our kindness. He is asking us to stop fixating on fickle, temporary, petty pursuits and instead invest our lives in what really matters: people.

Help Desk

A few years ago my wife and I were at the airport in Bali, Indonesia. We were trying to find our gate, but no one spoke English. I was starting to panic a little. Then a minor miracle:

we came across a kiosk that had "Help Desk" written on it in English. There was a nicely dressed woman sitting behind the counter.

I ran up to the desk. "Excuse me, ma'am, could you help me?"

She looked at me. Then she looked past me. But she didn't say a word.

I was a bit confused, but I don't give up easily. I said it again, more loudly this time. "Ma'am, could you please help me?"

She looked back at me. Then she looked past me again. I couldn't believe it. She was completely ignoring me. I was a little upset at this point. "Ma'am, I'm lost. I'm desperate. Could I please get some help here?"

No response. She just stared blankly into the distance. I was really mad now.

DawnCheré said, "Babe, calm down."

I replied with righteous anger and holy zeal, "She's at the help desk! This is her *job*!"

A woman walking by saw the commotion and walked over to us. "Sir, do you need assistance?"

She speaks English! There is a God, I thought.

"Yes!" I said. "I need *help* finding my gate, so I came to the *Help* Desk, but I can't seem to get any *help*." I was emphasizing the word *help* because clearly, someone wasn't doing her job.

The woman who had approached me began speaking to the woman behind the desk in another language. Then she turned back to me. "Sir, this woman doesn't speak English. And, sir, she doesn't work here. She is just sitting here."

I remember thinking, *That's not okay! Why would you sit behind a desk that says "Help Desk" if you can't help me?*

Then it hit me. How many Christians take on the title of Jesus follower, but when the world looks for help, we don't speak their language, and we aren't on duty? Too often we are so distracted by our pursuit of greatness that we forget true greatness is simply helping people. They are standing before us, lost and hurting, desperate for help. They are looking to us for answers.

After Jesus went back to heaven, and in the years before Christians became known as Christians, Jesus followers were simply said to be part of "The Way." Jesus said he was the way, the truth, and the life (John 14:6). The way to what? To true joy, fulfillment, peace, greatness, salvation.

We need to see ourselves as people of the Way. We are followers of Jesus, and we know the way to him. We are called to find the broken, the hurting, and the disenfranchised. We are called to be their friends. We are called to serve them and to love them the way Jesus serves and loves us.

The path to greatness is service. We can't save anyone, but we can serve everyone. And as we serve them, Jesus will save them. As we love them, Jesus will heal them. As we bless them, Jesus will build them.

We aren't the answer, but we know the answer. Our calling is to serve people by showing them the way to Jesus. All of us can be great, because all of us can serve.

EPILOGUE

LOVE BETRAYED

YEARS AGO AMERICAN AIRLINES GAVE me Emerald Status. I guess it was their way of thanking me for spending large portions of my life trapped in a tube at thirty thousand feet. At the time I had no idea what Emerald Status meant. I just assumed I would get more frequent flyer miles or something.

Then someone who heard about it mentioned, "Hey, if you are ever in Melbourne, you should check out the Qantas First Class Lounge."

I've flown through Melbourne quite a bit, but I had never heard of this lounge. I said, "I don't usually fly first class, so I don't think I have access to that. They wouldn't let me in."

My friend assured me, "Yes, they will. You are Emerald Status, man. You have access."

A few months later I happened to fly through Melbourne with my friend Phil. I said, "Phil! I just remembered. There's something called the Qantas First Class Lounge here. Let's go see if we can get in. It could be fun!"

Phil said, "I don't know . . . we aren't in first class. But, yeah, let's give it a go."

We started following these small discreet signs through the airport. It was like a maze: there were stairs, elevators, and hallways. Finally, we came to a set of nondescript, closed doors. A tiny sign above said "Qantas First Class Lounge."

We were feeling a bit timid, but as we approached the doors, they suddenly swung open. We walked into a beautiful lobby, as far removed from the airport as heaven is from hell. There was a man behind a desk with a perfect smile and perfectly coifed hair. He was so well groomed he looked fake.

I said, "Sir, I've been told we have access to this lounge."

He said, "Let me see your ticket." He checked my ticket. He typed something into his computer. He looked up at my face, then down at his screen, then up at me again. Then he smiled and said, "Mr. Wilkerson, sir! We've been waiting for you! Enter at your leisure!" And he gestured inside.

Phil and I walked into the next room, and it was indeed heaven on earth. There were white leather couches. There was mood lighting. Art was hanging on the walls. There was free Internet. We even found a restaurant inside with a full breakfast menu. I glanced over it and my mouth watered: eggs Benedict, Belgian waffles, bacon. I tried to find the prices, but oddly, there were none listed. Then it hit me: it was all *free*. This place was unbelievable!

I looked at Phil and said, "Phil, isn't this crazy? All these years I've been coming to Melbourne, all the times I've been in this airport, I could have had access to this room. I could have been getting free bacon. I had no idea."

Right then I felt God speak to me. "Rich, that's what people do. They have access to heaven's throne. But some of them don't know that, and others don't believe that, so they stay outside. They are all welcome. They can enter at their leisure because Jesus is the way to me."

So often people try to do life alone. They believe in God, and they might even pray to God, but for some reason they think he is not on their side. They can't imagine God could be their friend.

My prayer throughout the pages of this book has been to show you how much Jesus loves you and how much he loves the world. But until you choose to believe and receive his love, you'll attempt to face life alone. Jesus is the friend of sinners. He's the friend of anyone and everyone who will accept his offer of friendship. And to those who accept it, he gives us access to the Father and to heaven.

It's one thing to agree mentally that Jesus wants to be the friend of sinners, but I think many of us disqualify ourselves before we even start that friendship. We assume that Jesus' friendship extends to everyone else, but since we know all the dirty details about ourselves, we assume we are excluded.

Maybe we don't do this with ourselves but instead do it with others. Again, I've tried to paint a picture throughout this book of Jesus' heart to draw all people to himself, regardless of their past, present, or future. We need to believe that even the people who seem furthest

> We need to believe that even the people who seem furthest from God are deeply loved by him and are being drawn by him.

from God are deeply loved by him and are being drawn by him. And maybe we are the ones who will lead them to him, if we are willing to be friends of sinners too.

I want to end with one final story from the Bible that illustrates Jesus' passionate desire to befriend the world. Nowhere is this desire clearer than in the events surrounding his arrest and crucifixion.

John 13 records Jesus' last meal with his disciples. It was a beautiful, moving moment, a time for his disciples to say goodbye to him. To this day, Christians everywhere remember the Last Supper when we participate in communion.

At the end of the meal, though, something unexpected and seemingly out of place happened. Jesus insisted on washing everyone's feet. In that culture, foot-washing was considered a lowly, menial task. It was completely illogical that Jesus would lower himself to such a level.

Peter outright refused: "You shall never wash my feet."

Jesus pushed back: "Unless I wash you, you have no part with me" (verse 8).

He went around the circle, serving every person in the room. Then he told them, "Now that I, your Lord and Teacher, have washed your feet, you also should wash one another's feet. I have set you an example that you should do as I have done for you" (verses 14–15).

As we saw in the last chapter, Jesus is the greatest servant of all, and he asks us to serve one another as well. He was the friend of sinners, so he served sinners; now he asks us to do the same.

That's not the whole story, though. Have you ever stopped to realize Jesus even washed Judas's feet? Judas is the most famous traitor in human history. At this point in the narrative, he was already planning to betray Jesus. He was just waiting for the right moment. Jesus knew that, of course. He made several references to it during the meal. But he still washed Judas's feet.

I can't imagine doing that. I think I would have broken Judas's feet, not washed them. I would have said, "Your feet stink, and so does your soul." I would have run him out of the room with a few choice words.

Not Jesus. No matter who we are, what we've done, or what we're planning to do, Jesus is committed to us. He is passionate about pursuing us, about capturing our hearts.

But Judas was evil! you're probably thinking. *He was a bad person.*

Yes, but Jesus stays the same. His love knows no end. Jesus doesn't just *do* love; Jesus *is* love. He can't stop loving, because he can't deny himself. He pursues us even when his love has been betrayed.

> **Jesus doesn't just *do* love; Jesus *is* love.**

The height of Judas's evil only proves the depth of Jesus' love. Judas's scandalous betrayal only highlights Jesus' scandalous grace.

The Bible is full of examples of God pursuing people who didn't deserve his love. He chased after people who had committed the worst mistakes imaginable, because he is the friend of sinners, and that's what he does.

He pursued Moses with a burning bush even after he murdered a man.

He pursued Rahab with a scarlet cord even after she had been a prostitute.

He pursued Gideon with an angel even after he had been terrified.

He pursued David with a prophet from God even after he committed adultery and murder.

He pursued Jonah with a fish even after he disobeyed the word of the Lord.

He pursued Lazarus with resurrection power even after he had been in the tomb for four days.

He pursued Peter with a beach breakfast even after he had denied him three times.

He pursued Thomas with nail-scarred hands even after he had doubted him.

He pursued Paul with a blinding light from heaven even after he had killed Jesus' followers.

And he pursued Judas by washing his feet even as his love was being betrayed.

Do you realize the extent of Jesus' love for you? Can you see and believe his love for sinners, for the world, for humanity? Or do you think you are the exception to his love? That your sins are too great, your love too weak, or your mistakes too many for Jesus to want you? Jesus is in hot pursuit of your heart. He is chasing you. Nothing you could do could change his passion for you.

By the same token, he is passionate about others. Even about the people we would tend to discount or disqualify. Jesus loves them, and he wants you and me to reach out to them, to accept them, to befriend them.

A few hours after the Last Supper, Jesus was in the Garden of Gethsemane with his disciples. He knew his time had come to be arrested. In the distance, he saw Judas and a crowd of soldiers and thugs coming toward him.

Judas stepped forward to greet Jesus. He kissed him, which in that culture should have been a sign of friendship—but it wasn't this time. Judas had previously told the men with him, "The one I kiss is the man; arrest him" (Matthew 26:48).

At that moment, Jesus said something I still cannot comprehend: "Do what you came for, friend" (verse 50). Wait, what? Friend? Why would Jesus choose that term? He knew what was happening. He knew the rejection, the greed, the hatred in Judas's heart. He knew the pain that lay ahead as a result of this betrayal. And yet he still called Judas *friend*.

Can you imagine what Judas felt when he heard that? *Jesus, you call me friend? Don't you know I'm betraying you? Don't you know I'm rejecting you? This doesn't make sense. You're supposed to hate me.*

It would end up being the last thing Jesus said to Judas. Less than twenty-four hours later, consumed with guilt, Judas committed suicide. Meanwhile, Jesus was led to the cross to die for the sins of humanity, the ultimate proof of his friendship with sinners.

Jesus loved Judas all the way to the end, and he loves us with the same passion, the same constancy, the same commitment. His message of unconditional friendship to sinners is the foundation of our walk with him.

I am so glad our love for God doesn't dictate his love for us. Our

> **His message of unconditional friendship to sinners is the foundation of our walk with him.**

love is fickle, but his love is faithful. Jesus pursued us when we were dead in our sins. He came to us. He convinced us of his love. He cleansed us and restored us.

He will never give up on us. He will never stop loving us. He is the friend of sinners, and when we accept his friendship, his love, and his grace, we become friends for all eternity.

ABOUT THE AUTHOR ·

PASTOR RICH WILKERSON JR. IS A dynamic communicator with a passion to encourage and inspire this generation. He and his wife, DawnCheré, pastor VOUS Church in Miami. VOUS Church is a catalyst for faith, creativity, and diversity that celebrates the unique culture of its vibrant city. Rich is the founder of VOUS Conference and author of *Sandcastle Kings: Meeting Jesus in a Spiritually Bankrupt World.*

NOTES

INTRODUCTION
1. Oscar Wilde, *A Woman of No Importance*, Act III, 1893.

CHAPTER 2: MORE THAN PANTS
1. C. S. Lewis, *Mere Christianity*, rev. ed. (New York: HarperCollins, 2009), 52.
2. Tim Keller, *Encounters with Jesus: Unexpected Answers to Life's Biggest Questions* (New York: Penguin Books, 2013), 37.

CHAPTER 8: WELCOME TO THE NEIGHBORHOOD
1. Michael Craven, "The Christian Conquest of Pagan Rome," Crosswalk.com, 2012, http://www.crosswalk.com/blogs/michael -craven/the-christian-conquest-of-pagan-rome-11640691.html.

CHAPTER 9: COMFORTABLY UNCOMFORTABLE
1. Kevin Carter, "Starving Child and Vulture," *Time* 100 Photos Series, 1993, http://100photos.time.com/photos/kevin-carter -starving-child-vulture.

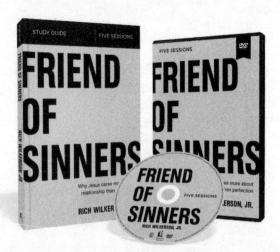

The Bible tells us that Jesus was called a lot of names by people. Many of the religious leaders of the day were jealous of his success and wanted to discredit him in the eyes of the public, so they said all sorts of crazy things about him. They whispered that he was an illegitimate child. They accused him of being demon-possessed. They denounced him to the Roman authorities as a rioter and a threat to public peace.

In this five-session video study, pastor and author Rich Wilkerson Jr. reveals how one of their nicknames for Jesus was true: "Here is a . . . friend of tax collectors and sinners" (Luke 7:34). In the religious leaders' minds this was one of the greatest indictments imaginable, but for Jesus it was a sign of success because it was the very definition of his mission. Today, Jesus still calls us "friends" not because of who we are or what we have done, but because of who he is. While he was on earth, he knew that people needed to feel as if they belonged before they would want to behave.

Rich shows that by following Jesus' example, we can have the same clear conviction and compassion for the lost that he did. When we embrace the truth that we all need Jesus equally and when we trust him to bring transformation in people's hearts, we will walk as Jesus walked, experiencing the glory of God in our own lives and in the lives of those around us.

The *Friend Of Sinners Study Guide* includes video discussion questions, Bible exploration, and personal study and reflection materials for in-between sessions.

Sessions include:
1. Missed Message
2. Weight Shift
3. Lost and Found
4. Comfortably Uncomfortable
5. How to Be Great

FRIEND OF SINNERS STUDY GUIDE WITH DVD
Why Jesus Cares More About Relationship Than Perfection

9780310095736